The Antislavery Move Ken

LOWELL H. HARRISON

THE UNIVERSITY PRESS OF KENTUCKY

Publication of this volume was made possible in part by a grant from the National Endowment for the Humanities.

Editorial and Sales Offices: The University Press of Kentucky
663 South Limestone Street, Lexington, Kentucky 40508-4008
www.kentuckypress.com

08 07 06 05 04 5 4 3 2 1

Library of Congress Cataloging-in-Publication Data

Harrison, Lowell Hayes, 1922-
   The antislavery movement in Kentucky.
   Bibliography: p.
   1. Slavery in the United States–Kentucky–Antislavery
movements. 2. Kentucky–History–1792-1865.
I. Title.
E445.K5H37   322.4'4'09769   77-92923
ISBN 0-8131-9083-5 (paper)

This book is printed on acid-free recycled paper meeting
the requirements of the American National Standard
for Permanence in Paper for Printed Library Materials.

Manufactured in the United States of America.

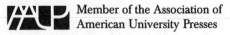 Member of the Association of
American University Presses

Contents

TO THE HARVEYS AND THE NATIONS

Preface

WHEN THE Civil War started in 1861, slavery existed in fifteen states. By the time the Thirteenth Amendment abolished it in December 1865, only Kentucky and Delaware still clung to the discredited institution. Yet from the inception of statehood some Kentuckians had opposed the system of human bondage that contradicted the principle of liberty enunciated in the Declaration of Independence only a few years earlier. While the Kentucky opponents of slavery were never able to secure its eradication through state action, they kept the issue alive and under discussion until slavery was at last ended by the constitutional amendment. A crusader does not have to achieve his goal to merit recognition for his efforts.

It is the purpose of this brief study to trace the development of the antislavery movement in Kentucky. Since slavery and antislavery are inexorably bound together, I have examined some aspects of slavery in Kentucky as an introduction to the antislavery movement. It might be more accurate to refer to "movements," for the opponents of slavery were never able to agree upon the best way to reach their goal. A chasm separated the advocates of abolition and emancipation. The terms were often used interchangeably until the 1820s, but thereafter they represented different approaches to the termination of slavery. While there were subtle differences within each group, abolitionists were likely to demand an immediate, uncompensated end to slavery; emancipationists were more likely to favor a gradual termination, perhaps with some compensation to the owners. To avoid confusion, I have maintained this distinction between the terms throughout the manuscript.

The topics of Kentucky slavery and antislavery attracted my

interest many years ago, and I have touched upon them in previous works. Much of my research has been done in the Library of Congress, the National Archives, the New York Public Library, the Antiquarian Society, and the Lexington Public Library. I owe particular thanks to the staffs of the Kentucky Library and the Helm-Cravens Library at Western Kentucky University, The Filson Club, the Kentucky State Historical Society, the Special Collections of the Margaret I. King Library of the University of Kentucky, the Special Collections at Berea College, and the Army War College Library, Carlisle Barracks, Pennsylvania. For their assistance I am deeply grateful.

1

THE PECULIAR
INSTITUTION

SLAVERY EXISTED IN Kentucky from the earliest days of settlement, and some slaves may have accompanied the hunters
who explored the area before 1775. One of the state's pioneers
recalled in later years that the first child born to the settlers in
Kentucky was "a coloured male child of a black woman in the
Family of Dr. N. Hart" at Boonesborough. When Daniel
Boone was marking the Wilderness Trail in 1775 his party was
attacked by Indians who killed Captain William Twetty and his
Negro servant. Colonel Richard Henderson's party that followed Boone included several slaves. During the late winter
of 1775–1776 Benjamin Logan brought his family from the
Holston settlements through the wilderness to the tiny station
of Saint Asaph's. His family included a female slave, Molly,
and her three sons, Matt, Dave, and Isaac. A decade later the
Logans owned fourteen slaves.[1] In the spring of 1777 Captain
John Cowan made a count of the inhabitants of Harrod's Fort,
then the largest settlement in Kentucky. Of the 198 people
listed, 19 were slaves, 7 of them children under ten years of
age.[2] The other small settlements probably contained other
slaves.

Monk Estill, the property of Captain James Estill of Madison County, was one of the most famous slaves in pioneer
Kentucky. Captured by Indians while his master was away on

a scouting expedition, Monk gave an exaggerated account of the station's strength which dissuaded the warriors from attacking. As the Indians retreated, Captain Estill and some twenty-five men intercepted them at Small Mountain Creek. During the desperate engagement that followed, the whites heard Monk's encouraging shouts: "Don't give way, Marse Jim; there's only twenty-five of the Injuns and you can whip them!" Captain Estill was killed in savage hand-to-hand combat, but Monk escaped and carried one of the wounded whites to safety. Given his freedom for his services, Monk was one of the first free blacks in Kentucky.[3]

Until 1830 the blacks in Kentucky increased at a faster rate than the whites. When the first federal census was taken in 1790, the area that would soon become Kentucky contained 73,077 inhabitants. Slaves numbered 11,830 or 16.2 percent. In 1830 the 165,213 slaves constituted 24 percent of the total population. Thereafter, the slave increase was less than that for whites, so that by 1860 the 225,483 slaves made up only 19.5 percent of the population. While free blacks had increased to 10,684 in 1860, they still numbered less than 1 percent.[4]

Kentucky's Population, 1790–1860

	Whites	Slaves	Free Blacks
1790	61,133 (83.7%)	11,830 (16.2%)	114 (0.2%)
1800	179,871 (81.7%)	40,343 (18.3%)	741 (0.3%)
1810	324,237 (79.8%)	80,561 (19.8%)	1,713 (0.4%)
1820	434,644 (77.0%)	126,732 (22.5%)	2,759 (0.5%)
1830	517,787 (75.3%)	165,213 (24.0%)	4,917 (0.7%)
1840	590,253 (75.7%)	182,258 (23.4%)	7,317 (0.9%)
1850	761,413 (77.5%)	210,981 (21.5%)	10,011 (1.0%)
1860	919,484 (79.6%)	225,483 (19.5%)	10,684 (0.9%)

One reason for the relative decline of slaves was the state's Non-Importation Act of 1833, but several other factors were also involved. Slaves could not legally be imported into the country after 1808, while in the 1840s and 1850s there was unusually heavy white immigration from Ireland and Germany. The greatest demand for slaves in Kentucky came during the early years when the region was being opened for settlement—when fields were being cleared, homes built, barns constructed, fences erected, all at the same time. After this initial period slave labor was in less demand, although some slaves were employed in a variety of small industrial enterprises. Tobacco, corn, cattle, and hemp were not so well suited to exploitation of mass labor as were cotton and sugarcane. Many Kentucky slaveholders concluded that slavery was not profitable, and thousands of slaves were exported to meet the insatiable demand of the Lower South for more and more workers. The Non-Importation Act may have been passed in part because some Kentuckians concluded that the state had a surplus of slaves.

Throughout the antebellum years the large majority of Kentucky whites were not slaveholders. In 1850, for example, when the white population was 761,413, only 38,385 owned slaves. Obviously, however, many people who did not own slaves were closely associated with the institution, and a more meaningful figure is the number of slaveholding families. Of 139,920 white families listed in the 1850 census, 28 percent held slaves. Of the 38,385 individual slaveholders, only 5 held over 100 slaves; no Kentuckian held as many as 200. Eighty-eight percent of the owners held fewer than 20, and 24 percent owned only one slave. Among the slave states in 1850, only Missouri averaged fewer slaves (4.5) per owner than Kentucky (5.4); the average South Carolina slaveholder owned 15. While eight states had more slaves than Kentucky, only Virginia (55,063) and Georgia (38,456) had more owners than did Kentucky in 1850. Robert Wickliffe, Sr., with nearly 200 slaves was reputed to be the state's largest owner in the early 1850s. Brutus J. Clay, brother of the renowned emancipationist, Cassius M. Clay, owned 132 slaves in 1860.[5] Such owners exerted an influence far out of proportion to their numbers.

Slaves were distributed unevenly across the state. In 1860, slaves comprised more than 30 percent of the population in 21 of Kentucky's 109 counties, Woodford County with 52 percent

3

having the largest concentration. Most of the largest slave-holding counties were in the Bluegrass, but Henderson and Oldham counties were pockets of heavy concentration on the Ohio River, and Trigg, Christian, Todd, and Warren counties formed a chain of high percentage slave counties across the southcentral portion of the state. Although Jefferson County's slave population was only 12 percent, its total population was so large that the 10,304 slaves in 1860 gave that county the largest number of slaves. Fayette County, with a much smaller total population, had 10,015 slaves.

On the other hand, in 23 counties the 1860 slave population was less than 5 percent of the total. Every county contained some slaves, but Jackson had only 7 in a population of 3,087. Most of the counties with low slave populations were in the mountainous eastern and southeastern parts of the state; there were also some areas of low concentration in the extreme northern and westcentral sections. In large sections of the commonwealth, most citizens had little direct contact with the peculiar institution.[6]

When Kentucky became a state in 1792, both constitutional and legislative provisions for slavery reflected the Virginia heritage. A requirement for separation was that slavery not be disturbed, and George Nicholas, the leader in the constitutional convention that met at Danville in April 1792, saw to the inclusion of an article affirming the institution in the final document. In his first message Governor Isaac Shelby asked the legislature to enact a slave code. "Your humanity as well as your duty," he said, "will induce you to pass laws to compel the proper treatment of slaves agreeable to the directions of the Constitution."[7] The early legislatures passed several laws pertaining to slavery, but a comprehensive slave code was not drafted until 1798. Somewhat milder than the Virginia code, it remained relatively intact until slavery was ended. Most of its provisions were similar to those of codes in other slave states, but Kentucky slaves accused of capital crimes against whites were given the benefit of a jury trial.

Later a number of acts were passed to supplement the code. In 1811, for example, slave crimes were specifically defined

4

and punishments provided. Punishment posed a problem, for few slaves could be fined and jail would deprive their masters of their services. Almost by default, whipping was the punishment most often prescribed. The 1811 law made four crimes punishable by death: conspiracy and rebellion, the administration of poison with intent to kill, voluntary manslaughter, and the rape of a white woman. Other crimes were later added to the list, and by 1860 eleven were included. By contrast, there were only four capital crimes for whites.

As the slave population increased and the need for slaves declined, many Kentucky slaveholders found themselves facing the economic danger of becoming "slave poor." Unlike free laborers, a slave could not be discharged or laid off when his services were not needed; the cost of maintaining a slave in idleness was almost as much as when he was at heavy labor. One solution was to sell the surplus; another was to hire out the extra hands.

When John Breckinridge began to develop his Bluegrass plantation in 1793, he refused to raise the tobacco that had ravaged his Virginia fields. His goal of a horse farm with diversified crops did not require extensive labor. But Breckinridge would not sell any of his slaves, and between 1793 and 1806 their number increased from twenty-five to fifty-seven. His solution was to hire out the slaves who were not needed at Cabell's Dale. Jim and George, his skilled carpenters, were available at $1 each per day for brief periods, but most of the agreements were for a year or more. In 1801 Peter January, a prominent Lexington businessman, agreed to employ six young male slaves for four years in his rope factory. In 1801 when Breckinridge prepared to take his seat in the Senate, he listed nineteen slaves available for hire.[8]

Slaves occasionally shared in the income from their labors. The Bowling Green city government frequently attempted to curb masters who allowed slaves to hire themselves out as if they were free. An ordinance of 1856 provided that an offending slave could be put to work for the town or hired out for the town's benefit for three months; in 1861 a fine of $40 was added to the penalty. In 1849 frugal housewife Elizabeth

5

Underwood wrote her husband that she had decided not to hire Dr. Ogden's Ben because the asking price of $100 to be paid to Ogden and $25 for Ben was too high.[9] In many communities January 1 was the traditional day for hiring slaves, and large crowds of slaveholders, prospective employers, and curious bystanders congregated at the county seat. A slave was sometimes allowed to veto a proposed deal, and in some cases the slave could return to his master if he objected to his treatment. But such discretion was not required, and it was not usually part of an agreement.

Most slaveholders did not hesitate to sell slaves when it was to their economic advantage, and the settlement of estates often necessitated the disposal of slaves who would never have been sold by their masters. As Kentucky acquired a surplus of slaves, the opening of new cotton and sugarcane lands in the Lower South created a profitable trade "down the river." A slave purchased in Kentucky for perhaps $800 could be carried to New Orleans for $50; there he might bring $1,000 to $1,200 on the auction block. Of course the price of slaves varied widely, depending upon such factors as age, health, sex, and particular skills. Prices also fluctuated according to general economic conditions. The Panic of 1837 saw the price of slaves decline sharply for several years, but for the period 1790–1860 the general trend was upward. H. T. Duncan of Lexington was almost embarrassed by the price of slaves in 1858. "Today I sold Sue and her Boy Noah about ten years of age for $1,700," he wrote a son on October 21. "Slaves are in more demand & for higher prices than I have ever known. She gets a good home in the neighborhood. Had I have sold her to go below I could have got 1900 or 2000. I am offered 400 cash for Amanda as worthless a Negro as lives. I ask 700 & expect to get it. I am anxious myself to dispose of every one I do not absolutely need. Indeed it would be better to let them all slide and put my estate in grass."[10]

Miscegenation, more common than many slaveholders liked to admit but less prevalent than many abolitionists claimed, resulted in some of the most heartrending tales of slaves who were sold. Such a case stirred Lexington in the mid-1850s. A

6

wealthy, respected white man was the father of two nearly white girls; their mother was his quadroon slave. Reared in comfort by their father, the girls were educated in Ohio where they attended Oberlin College. They passed easily as whites, but their legal status was well known in Lexington. Financial reverses placed the father heavily in debt, and when his daughters came to Lexington to attend his funeral they were seized and ordered sold for the benefit of creditors of the estate. Despite public indignation over the girls' plight, the law ran its course. They were subjected to the humiliation of a public auction and lascivious examination by prospective buyers, and they were sold to a New Orleans gambler who later resold them as mistresses to a wealthy purchaser.[11]

For every such incident hundreds of slaves were sold without arousing a public outcry. Many Kentuckians accepted sales as an inevitable part of the institution of slavery, although the dissolution of families was an unpleasant aspect. Some masters refused to break up families, but others who had scruples were able to overcome them if the price was high enough. The *Bardstown Candid Review* for June 20, 1809, carried a notice from Luidores Lucas: "The subscriber has for sale a negro man and woman, each 24 years of age, both are excellent plantation hands, together with two children. They will be sold separately or altogether." But a Lexington paper of January 28, 1835, showed a quite different approach: "For Sale. A negro man, a first rate farm hand, about 27 years of age; and a very likely woman, the wife of the man, about 22 years of age, a good house servant. They will not be sold separately, or to any person wishing to take them out of the state."[12]

One consequence of the possible breakup of families was the temporary nature of marital arrangements. Some slave marriages were sanctified by having the couple step over a broom; some included "until death or sale do us part" in the informal vows. The Beaver Dam Baptist Church was confronted with an unusual problem in February 1830, when "Brother Peter a man of culler being deprived of the society of his wife by removal from this country and being desirous to have a companion request the advice of the church on that subject." The subject was twice postponed, and in April Brother Peter asked that his case be dropped.[13] One can only wonder what arrangements he had made.

While numerous slaves were sold within the state, the major market was in the Lower South. It is impossible to ascertain how many slaves were exported from the state. Robert Wickliffe, Sr., asserted in the legislature in 1840 that over 60,000 slaves had been sold out-of-state during the preceding seven years, but his estimate was much too large.[14] Frederic Bancroft, whose *Slave-Trading in the Old South* remains the basic study of that subject, estimated that Kentucky's annual exports averaged 2,323 in the 1830s, perhaps 2,000 in the 1840s and 3,400 in the 1850s.[15]

Even some slaveholders scorned the slave traders who carried on that distasteful aspect of slavery, and some traders operated clandestinely to preserve their social respectability. A student at Western Military Institute in Georgetown explained in 1848 why he was breaking up with his roommate. In addition to "some short words" that had been exchanged, William Preston Johnston wrote indignantly, "I did not know when I went to room with him, that he was the son of a negro trader."[16]

Other traders were quite open in their dealings, and some occupied a respectable place in their communities. As early as July 1816, Edward Stone, who lived near Paris, advertised for twenty male and female slaves between ten and twenty-five years of age. Lexington became the center of the state's slave trade, although small traders, who usually conducted some other business as well, operated throughout the state. The large slave trader with his crowded slave pens and shuffling coffles of blacks most offended public sensibilities. Robert Wickliffe, Sr., called upon the 1840 legislature to stop "the abominable traffic . . . the horrid practice of *driving them like cattle to market*. . . ." It was, he declared angrily and futilely, a great blot on the moral character of Kentuckians.[17]

The traffic was not halted. In 1843 the firm of Hughes and Downing opened in Lexington, and their success with their first group of slaves explains why opponents were not able to

8

eradicate the trade. During the fall of 1843 the partners purchased six girls and seven boys for $5,292.50. After expenses of $257.42, the slaves sold in Natchez in early 1844 for $8,695, leaving Hughes and Downing a profit of $3,145.08.[18] They were not likely to heed Wickliffe's strictures to abandon the trade.

Before 1850 Lewis C. Robards was the state's best-known slave trader. His advertisements for slaves ran regularly in Bluegrass newspapers, and in 1849 he leased the Lexington slave jail of William A. Pullum, whose poor health forced him into retirement. As his business expanded, Robards first leased and then purchased a former theater that he converted into a larger slave jail. His "choice stock" of lovely girls was segregated in luxurious second-floor apartments; the downstairs slaves, destined for quick sale, enjoyed less comfortable quarters. Robards often purchased diseased slaves whose ailments were not readily visible, doctored them up, and then sold them at full price to unwary purchasers. As a consequence of such practices, he was involved in frequent lawsuits and was often threatened by irate customers. Robards offered to board slaves for twenty-five cents a day and to sell them for 2½ percent commission. Economic setbacks put Robards in debt, and in 1855 his quarters and some of his slaves were sold to satisfy the claims of creditors.

The purchaser was the firm of Bolton, Dickens, & Company, by then Kentucky's largest slave-trading company, with branch offices in Memphis, Charleston, Natchez, Saint Louis, and New Orleans. In October 1855 this firm advertised for "200 likely YOUNG NEGROES of both sexes." By 1858 over two dozen slave traders and companies were advertising in the Lexington papers, and the "Athens of the West" was described as "one of the largest slave markets in the United States." Louisville also developed an extensive slave market with the Arteburn brothers, Jordan and Tarlton, probably the best-known dealers. But the Louisville market was not as successful as the Lexington one.[19]

Almost no one said anything favorable about the slave trade, but there were wide disagreements about other aspects of

9

slavery. Although some modern scholars challenge their assertion, many contemporary observers of slavery, including some opponents of it, agreed that the institution was milder and more humane in Kentucky than in the Lower South. James Silk Buckingham, a British abolitionist who saw slavery in several states, commented that "there is no doubt that in Kentucky their condition is very much better than in most other states, their work lighter, their food and clothing better, and their treatment more kind and humane." The Reverend John Rankin, who devoted much of his life to combating slavery, said that slavery wore its "mildest aspect" in Kentucky.[20] He could have pointed out by way of example that Kentucky was one of only three slave states where the education of slaves was not legally prohibited. A considerable number of the state's slaves learned to read, despite fears that they might be contaminated by abolitionist propaganda. Fewer were taught to write, for that skill opened up too many possibilities for forged passes.

While the slave code of 1798 and its later modifications placed many restrictions upon slaves and their activities, some laws were designed to protect them, although in practice these laws were often not enforced. An act passed in 1830 provided, "If any owner of a slave shall treat such slave cruelly, so as in the opinion of the jury, to endanger the life or limb of such slave, or shall not supply his slave with sufficient food or raiment," the ill-treated slave could be taken from the owner and sold, the revenue being given to the owner.[21] In an 1838 case Judge J. Ewing ruled that slaves were property, "and must under our present institutions, be treated as such. But they are human beings, with like passions, sympathies and affections with ourselves. . . ."[22]

Blacks were not allowed to testify against whites, and most whites were reluctant to push a case against another white on behalf of a slave, but in a few outrageous instances public sentiment demanded action. One sensational case involved Caroline A. Turner, wife of retired Judge Fielding L. Turner of Lexington. The judge acknowledged that his wife had killed six slaves by severe beatings, and in 1837 the violent-tempered Mrs. Turner crippled a small Negro boy by throwing him out of a second-floor window. To protect his wife against prosecution, Judge Turner had her committed to the lunatic asylum. Authorities released her, however, before the hearing that she demanded. When the judge died in 1843 he left all his slaves to his children. "None of them are to go to the said Caroline, for it would be to doom them to misery in life & a speedy death." But Mrs. Turner contested the will and secured several slaves. In August 1844, while she was happily whipping Richard, he tore loose from his chains and strangled her. Despite his provocation, Richard had committed an unpardonable sin for a slave, and he was hanged on November 19.[23]

A slave's economic value provided more protection than slave laws, for he represented a substantial capital investment. Laws that prohibited the freeing of a slave likely to become a public charge were well enforced, and only an enraged or foolish master would inflict punishment that resulted in serious injury. Even a temporary incapacity was an economic loss, and numerous farm and plantation records show the slaves being treated by the same physician who cared for the white family. Many travelers in the Old South reported seeing whites employed in the most dangerous work. Lose an Irishman and hire another; lose a slave and the loss was serious.

Slavery violated a fundamental human right to freedom, and its defenders had difficulty in justifying the institution. But given the existence of slavery, a pertinent question was how well the slaves were treated within its framework. The answers were so different that respondents might have been describing entirely different systems. By careful selection of cases, one could "prove" anything about slavery. Given the wide discretion enjoyed by the master, the truest statement that can be made about the treatment of Kentucky slaves is that it depended largely upon the individual master. An elderly ex-slave summed up the matter well when he said years later: "Some slaves were treated good, and some were treated awful bad by the white people; but most of them were treated good if they would do what their masters told them to do."[24]

The state's most notorious instance of cruelty to slaves was the famous case of Lilburne and Isham Lewis, nephews of Thomas Jefferson. Slaves frequently attempted to escape from the harsh treatment at their "Rocky Point" plantation in Livingston County. On a December evening in 1811, during a bout of heavy drinking, the brothers decided to make an example of seventeen-year-old George, who had run away at least twice. While the assembled slaves watched in horror, George was bound to a heavy meat block and chopped to bits that were tossed into the fire. Subsequent discovery of his bones lent substance to rumors, and in 1812 the brothers were indicted by the county grand jury. Learning of their impending arrest, they agreed to a suicide pact, but Lilburne shot himself accidentally before the posse arrived. Isham was sentenced to hang but escaped before the execution day. What happened to him is uncertain, but a judge ordered the case dropped in 1815 because the defendant was reported dead.[25]

Many ex-slaves denied personal knowledge of cruel punishments. Harriet Mason said of her slavery days, "There was no jail on the place, and I never saw a slave whipped or punished in any way." Wes Woods echoed her recollections: "I never saw a slave whipped or in chains. My boss didn't believe in that kind of punishment. If the children needed whipping it was done like all other children are whipped when they need it." Dan Bogie often played with Rube, the son of his master, "and when we acted bad old Marse always licked Rube three or four times harder than he did me because Rube was older."[26]

But there was also much evidence on the other side. Edd Shirley said that slaves who obeyed orders were treated well, but he recalled that "I onced saw a light colored gal tied to the rafters of a barn, and her master whipped her until blood ran down her back and made a large pool on the ground." Joana Owens's master was Nolan Barr, who owned a large farm near Hawesville, and "when the old master got mad at his slaves for not working hard enough he would tie them up by their thumbs and whip the male slaves till they begged for mercy." In her old age Sophia Word delighted to claim that "the white folks said I was the meanest nigger that ever wuz." Her mistress dragged her into the house one day, Sophia chuckled: "Then I grabs that white woman, when she turned her back, and shook her until she begged for mercy. When the master comes in, I wuz given a terrible beating with a whip but I didn't care. . . ." But, she continued, "My master wuzn't as mean as most masters. Hugh White wuz so mean to his slaves that I know of two gals that killt themselfs."[27]

Whippings were the usual punishment employed by the master, as they were by the state. When a slave was branded or had his ears cropped, it was more often for the purpose of identifying a persistent runaway or troublemaker than as a punishment. For intractable slaves sale was a form of permanent punishment.

Since Kentucky had few large plantations, the care of slaves was less formalized than on some of the large plantations in the Lower South. The typical Kentucky slaveholder was in close contact with his few slaves, and his attention to food, clothing, and shelter was based on his observations and the slaves' requests. How well their needs were met depended upon him and his available resources.

Basic rations ran heavily to the three m's—meat, meal, and molasses—but most masters encouraged slaves to raise a garden and to supplement their diets by hunting and fishing. Except in unusual circumstances, hunting was done without guns. Dan Bogie recalled the gastronomical aspect of slave days with obvious delight. "Most of the cooking was done in an oven in the yard, over a bed of coals," he explained. "Baked possum and ground hog in the oven, stewed rabbits, fried fish and fried bacon called 'streaked meat,' all kinds of vegetables, boiled cabbage, pone corn bread, and sorghum molasses. Old folks would drink coffee, but children would drink milk, especially buttermilk." Some venturesome slaves tried to share the master's diet. "We lived tobly well and didn't starve for we had enough to eat, but we didn't have as good as the master and the mistress had," said Sophia Word who was born into slavery in 1837. "We would slip in the house after the master and mistress wuz sleeping and cook to suit ourselves. . . ."[28]

13

Some masters handed out delicacies such as candy and oranges at Christmas and other special occasions.

Clothing loomed less large in the memories of ex-slaves than food. Household slaves often wore hand-me-downs of the white family unless the estate was sufficiently affluent to boast its own livery. Most slaves wore rough, serviceable garments, many of them homemade. "The family all wore home made clothing," said ex-slave Will Oats, "cotton shirts, heavy shoes, very heavy underwear; and if they wore out their winter shoes before the spring weather they had to do without until fall."[29]

Some household slaves lived in the "big house," and on large plantations most lived in quarters close enough to the overseer for close supervision. On a typical Kentucky farm with only a few slaves the quarters probably consisted of a one-room-and-loft log cabin, although a lean-to might be added for a large family. Furniture was sparse and often crudely made—a bed or two, a trundle bed underneath, a table, some benches or chairs. Stoves were rare; cooking was usually done at a fireplace or outdoors. Some owners prided themselves upon having brick, stone, or frame slave houses, but such elaborate structures were exceptions. Most Kentucky slaves were on farms, but the ones in urban areas lived in close proximity with the white family. Housing segregation was not common in such towns as Louisville and Lexington.

Despite the hard labor that usually accompanied slavery, slaves found opportunities for amusement. Masters often encouraged recreation, for contented slaves did more and better work than unhappy ones. Hunting and fishing provided good sport as well as food, and work itself gave an excuse for congenial gatherings, as it always had on the American frontier. Dan Bogie remembered, "We did not work on Saturday afternoon. The men would go fishing and the women would go to the neighbors and help each other piece quilts. We used to have big times at the corn shuckings. The neighbors would come and help. We would have camp fires and sing songs, and usually a big dance at the barn when the corn was shucked. Some of the slaves from other plantations would pick the banjo, then the dance."[30] Some masters might enliven such occasions by providing a jug or two, but others either opposed liquor on moral grounds or hesitated to subject slaves to its influence. Some masters encouraged community dances and parties while others sought to limit interplantation contacts in order to reduce the danger of slave plots and cooperative escapes.

Religion was important in the lives of many slaves, although the master's attitude was important in determining just what form worship would take. A common defense of slavery was that it brought Christianity to the heathen. If a black received the hope of life eternal, should he not willingly give his earthly services in return? Properly taught, religion should make the slave more content with his lot on earth by focusing his attention on the hereafter. But the haunting fear that any slave assemblage might result in plotting escape or insurrection often led whites to restrict the slaves' worship. Some communities allowed Negro churches and Negro ministers but required at least two white men to be present at each meeting. Other communities set aside the balcony or the rear pews of their churches for the slaves, but the entire congregation usually sang together, took communion together, and were subject to the same church discipline.

While some clergymen, some parishioners, and some churches opposed slavery, most of the Kentucky churches "reflected the society of which they were a part." Since each Baptist congregation was an autonomous body, it was easier for churches of that denomination to admit slaves to membership than it was for churches more restricted by hierarchical regulations. In July 1849, for example, the rolls of the South Benson Baptist Church in Franklin County showed 132 white and 98 black members.[31]

A number of black ministers became locally well known in Kentucky; they occupied the most important position usually open to a slave. John Ashburn, known as "John the Baptist," was owned by Henry Ashburn of Logan County. An observer who heard him twice in 1816–1817 reported that he preached with "great power and energy," and "on each occasion he had large congregations, composed of both black and white." One of his sermons concerned the need for slaves to obey their masters. In 1854 Landon Ferrell, a free black, was the minister of the 1,820-member First African Baptist Church in Lexington; it was then the largest church in the state.[32] Some whites feared the influence of Negro ministers, and in 1857 Senator George W. Silvertooth introduced a bill to prohibit Negroes from preaching in Kentucky. The proposal was referred to committee where it apparently died.

Slaves sometimes worshiped secretly, and even under white supervision they were sometimes able to develop a religious subculture that freed them to some degree from the dominance of their masters. Religion helped reconcile many slaves to their unfortunate status, and it probably reduced the likelihood of slave revolts. Religion helped the slave endure slavery.[33]

No aspect of slavery was examined more closely during the antebellum years than its economic value, for economics provided one of the institution's major defenses. But neither contemporary Kentuckians nor later historians could agree on slavery's economic importance to the state. Variables such as the replacement value of slaves were subject to such different assessments that calculations could give widely different results. Few slaveholders argued that investment in slaves was the most profitable use of capital. Despite his close involvement with the institution, Squire Turner asserted in the 1849 constitutional convention that 75 percent of Kentucky's slaves hardly met their expenses and that the rate of return on capital invested in slaves was no more than 3 percent. There was general agreement that corn, tobacco, hemp, and livestock were not as well suited for slave labor as cotton and sugarcane. Warner L. Underwood hoped to move to Mississippi where his slaves could raise cotton, "for they are entirely unprofitable in Kentucky. . . . it has more than taken all that the profitable ones could produce to support the old, the young, and the unproductive, so that I have supported my negroes and not they me."[34]

But many masters had inherited both their slaves and slavery as a way of life; wasn't it just like a Yankee abolitionist to measure everything by dollars and cents? There were some things that were more important than the maximum rate of return on capital invested. Many masters felt a genuine sense of responsibility toward their human property; what would happen to the aged, the young, the crippled, and infirm if slavery were ended as some thoughtless agitators demanded?

During the years before the Civil War, slavery in Kentucky experienced a decline in relative importance, and the flow of slaves to the Lower South suggested that slavery within the state was less profitable than it was elsewhere. The institution did not appear to be as firmly fastened upon Kentucky as it was in some of the other slave states, and some Kentuckians who deplored the presence of slavery sought to end it within the commonwealth.

2

THE EARLY
OPPOSITION

SLAVERY WAS already something of an anomaly at the time
of the American Revolution, although it existed in all thirteen
colonies. A number of Americans could not reconcile its existence with the ideas expressed in the Declaration of Independence. Other protests were made on economic and moral
grounds, and before the Revolution ended, several northern
states had provided for the end of slavery, sometimes on a
gradual basis that took decades to complete. The Northwest
Ordinance of 1787 prohibited slavery in the public domain
north of the Ohio River, with the result that Kentucky's long
northern boundary touched free territory for its entire length.
Thomas Jefferson led a determined but futile effort to abolish
slavery in Virginia; few of those who defeated his proposal defended slavery as a positive good. It was seen as an evil that
unfortunately had been forced upon the colony by Great Britain. Regrettably, there was no practical way of discarding it.

As Kentucky neared statehood, the need for a constitution
afforded Kentuckians an opportunity to determine the future
of slavery within the state. Those who opposed the institution
were led by "Father" David Rice, a Presbyterian minister
from Hanover County, Virginia, who had moved to Kentucky
in 1783 in search of souls to be saved and good land to be
purchased. He returned to Virginia after a brief stay, but a

petition signed by 300 people urged him to return to the western waters. Rice arrived in Danville in October 1783 and in less than a year organized three Presbyterian churches. A graduate of Princeton, he began teaching in the new Transylvania Seminary in 1787.[1] His opposition to slavery was well known, and when the convention call was issued he assumed leadership of the antislavery forces.

Three months before the convention assembled in Danville, Rice published a comprehensive attack on slavery in a pamphlet, "Slavery Inconsistent with Justice and Good Policy." A modern historian has hailed it as "the most comprehensive indictment of slavery to that time, one of the finest of all time. . . . a masterpiece of sustained argument."[2] Rice left no doubt about his basic point: "As creatures of God, we are, with respect to liberty, all equal." When a slave claimed freedom, "unless his master can prove that he is not a man, that he was not born free, or that he has forfeited or relinquished his freedom, he must be judged free, the justice of his claim must be acknowledged." Rice warned slaveholders of the danger of maintaining a group "whose interest it will be, whenever in their power, to subvert the government, and throw all into confusion."

Slavery was bad for the whites, Rice insisted; it "naturally tends to sap the foundations of moral, and consequently of political virtue. . . . [It] produces idleness, and idleness is the muse of vice." It corrupted youth by giving them a false sense of pride; wherever slavery became common, "industry sinks into disgrace." Rice predicted that if slavery should be abolished, five useful citizens would enter Kentucky for each slaveholder excluded.

"You say, a law of emancipation, would be unjust," he challenged his opponents, "because it would deprive men of their property; but is there no injustice on the other side? Is nobody entitled to justice, but slaveholders?" Balance one injustice against the other, Rice urged. "Shall we hesitate a moment to determine, who is the greatest sufferer, and who is treated with the greatest injustice?" Slavery led to so much miscegenation, he declared, that the nation would ultimately consist of mulattoes unless slavery was ended. In a learned scriptural argument he denied biblical sanction for the institution.

Slavery should be ended at once, Rice concluded; it would be foolish to wait until abolition was inevitable. "We may now do it in a peaceable manner, without going a step out of the way of our duty; and without hazarding what might be attended with tenfold more confusion and danger."

"The slavery of the Negro began in iniquity: a curse has attended it, and a curse will follow it," he asserted. "National vices will be punished with national calamities. Let us avoid these vices that we may avoid the punishment which they deserve; and endeavour so to act, as to secure the approbation and smiles of heaven."[3]

Had the convention heeded the Presbyterian Cassandra, Kentucky's history would have been much different. But as Abraham Lincoln remarked in an 1859 speech, "When the Kentuckians came to form the Constitution, they had the embarrassing circumstances of slavery among them—they were not a free people to make their Constitution."[4] Elected to the convention, Rice repeated his arguments there. Conceding that slavery could not be suddenly abolished, he urged the writing of a constitution that would reject slavery in principle and require the legislature to develop a plan for gradual emancipation. The importation of slaves should be halted, and a system of education should be installed so that slaves would become useful citizens when freed.

Rice did not wage the battle alone. The *Kentucky Gazette* carried some antislavery protests, and there were several opponents of slavery in the Baptist, Methodist, and Presbyterian churches. Rice was one of seven ministers in the 1792 convention, and all were antislavery. But the proslavery forces had both a majority of the votes and an outstanding leader in George Nicholas, then perhaps Kentucky's greatest lawyer, and they had their way.

Slavery was considered so important that a separate article (IX) was devoted to it. With only minor modifications in future constitutions, this article provided the legal basis for slavery in Kentucky for over seventy years.

"The legislature shall have no power to pass laws for the emancipation of slaves without the consent of their owners, or without paying their owners, previous to such emancipation, a full equivalent in money, for the slaves emancipated; they shall have no power to prevent immigrants to this state, from bringing with them such persons as are deemed slaves by the laws of any one of the United States, so long as any person of the same age or description shall be continued in slavery by the laws of this state; that they shall pass laws to permit the owners of slaves to emancipate them, saving the rights of creditors, and preventing them from becoming a charge to the county in which they reside; they shall have full power to prevent slaves from being brought into this state as merchandise; they shall have full power to prevent any slave being brought into this state from a foreign country, and to prevent those from being brought into this state, who have been since the first of January, 1789, or may hereafter be imported into any of the United States from a foreign country. And they shall have full power to pass such laws as may be necessary to oblige the owners of slaves to treat them with humanity, to provide for them necessary clothes and provisions, to abstain from all injuries to them extending to life or limb, and in case of their neglect or refusal to comply with the directions of such laws, to have such slave or slaves sold for the benefit of their owner or owners."

The opening sentence was the barrier against which antislavery advocates would spend their efforts. Perhaps in protest against the intent to make slavery perpetual, David Rice resigned from the convention on April 11. A week later when Samuel Taylor of Mercer County moved to delete Article IX, his motion was defeated 16–26.

Despite their initial defeat, the opponents of slavery continued to agitate the question. The Baptist General Committee of Virginia had taken a strong antislavery stand in 1788, and in 1789 the Rolling Fork Baptist Church in Nelson County asked the Salem Association, "Is it lawful in the sight of God for a member of Christ's church to keep his fellow creatures in perpetual slavery?" When the association failed to give the anticipated negative answer, the Rolling Fork Church severed its connection with the association. But by 1830 when this church was reorganized most of its members were slaveholders or slaves. A few other churches also withdrew from their associations, and an occasional church was antislavery from its inception. Some of them refused to admit slaveholders. Individuals also made known their protests. William Hickman, moderator of the Elkhorn Baptist Church, withdrew in 1807 "on account of the practice of slavery as being tolerated."[5]

But the antislavery sentiment among the Baptists should not be exaggerated; most churches and most members either approved of slavery or acquiesced in its existence. In 1805 the Elkhorn Association stated, "This Association Judges it improper for ministers Churches or Association to meddle with emancipation from slavery or any other political Subject and as such we advise ministers and Churches to have nothing to do therewith in their religious Capacities." In 1811 it was said that of 17,511 Kentucky Baptists there were only 300 members, twelve ministers, and twelve churches that were openly antislavery.[6]

The Methodist church also contained an antislavery element. Both John Wesley and Francis Asbury had denounced slavery, and the 1784 conference that formally organized the Methodist Church in the United States called upon each slaveholding member to free within a year his slaves who were forty to forty-five years of age and to provide for the gradual emancipation of the younger ones. Children born in slavery thereafter should be freed at birth. Anyone not complying should withdraw from the church or, after a year's grace, be expelled. But the complexities of the problems were revealed in an additional statement that negated much of the brave declaration: "These rules are to affect the members of our society no farther than as they are consistent with the laws of the states in which they reside." The rule was later suspended, and in 1796 the *Discipline* was amended to say that a slaveholder could not become a church member "till the preacher who has oversight of the circuit, has spoken to him freely and faithfully on the subject of slavery." Later, two *Disciplines* were printed, one for the North and one for the South, and in 1808 each conference was authorized to form its own rules regarding slavery.[7]

Some Kentucky Methodists continued to oppose slavery despite fears that such opposition cost the denomination the membership of many upper-class slaveholders. Ministers were often charged with "a wish to interfere with the civil institutions of the state. . . ." The Reverend John Ray tried to avoid staying at a home that had slaves, and Peter Cartwright moved to Illinois largely to escape the distasteful slavery atmosphere. But most Methodists either condoned slavery or refrained from attacking it. "What had the slaves gained," some Methodists seemed to ask, "if the Methodists, because of their abolitionism, were prevented from showing them the path to eternity?"[8]

The Presbyterian attitude was reflected in the case of David Rice, who fought to end slavery but never freed his own slaves. Many Presbyterians believed that slavery would soon disappear, probably as the consequence of another constitutional convention. In 1794 the Transylvania Presbytery, in anticipation of that day, ordered its slaveholders to teach slave children under fifteen to read and write and to "give them such education as may prepare them for the enjoyment of freedom." Since slavery was doomed to extinction anyway, there was no need to push the issue to the point of causing a denominational split. So the Transylvania Presbytery resolved in 1796 that "although Presbytery are fully convinced of the great evil of slavery, yet they view the final remedy as alone belonging to the civil power; and also do not think that they have sufficient authority from the word of God to make it a term of church communion." Slaveholders' consciences were further assuaged the next year by the declaration that while slavery was a moral evil, not all slaveholders were guilty of moral evil. During the early years of the nineteenth century the Presbyterians were generally more moderate in their opposition to slavery than were the Baptists or Methodists.[9] While individuals in other denominations were antislavery, the churches themselves were less hostile toward slavery than these three.

Opponents of slavery had another opportunity to seek its curtailment sooner than they could reasonably have anticipated. The 1792 constitution came under severe criticism even as it went into effect. While there were many detailed criticisms, a basic objection was that it was not sufficiently democratic, that it catered to the aristocratic element. The discontented began to press for another convention.

John Breckinridge was one of the "aristocrats" who feared economic loss from proposed changes. As he wrote Isaac Shelby, if "they can by one experiment emancipate our slaves [,] the same principle pursued will enable them at a second experiment to extinguish our land titles. . . ." Breckinridge worked tirelessly in 1798 to defeat the convention proposal. Opponents of slavery, he suggested sarcastically, could free their own slaves and "satiate their humanity" by buying and freeing slaves belonging to others. Slaves were property and property rights were sacred, he declared again and again. Yet he conceded that the principle of emancipation might be acceptable.[10] George Nicholas and other conservative slaveholders joined in the campaign. Young Henry Clay, newly arrived in Kentucky, called for a future scheme of gradual emancipation through ordinary legislative procedure, but his ardor for emancipation dissipated as he realized that his proposal might blight his political future.

Despite the conservative opposition and the cumbersome procedure for calling a convention, a majority of the voters provided for a convention in 1799. Breckinridge, Nicholas, and their cohorts then worked to elect delegates who would be sound on such key issues as emancipation. The dissidents were badly underrepresented in the convention, for they did not organize their campaign as well as did their opponents. The majority of the fifty-five delegates were in such agreement that the constitution was written in less than a month. The slavery provisions of 1792 were transferred almost intact to Article VII of the new document, and no scheme of emancipation was included. Kentucky had a constitution that would last for fifty years.

The dispute over calling a convention did result in a spirited discussion of slavery, and it was significant that opponents voiced their opposition freely. A Scott County meeting on March 30, 1799, touched off much of the controversy with a resolution: "That Slavery, as it now exists in this state, is a great national evil, and incompatible with a free government, and ought to be abolished as soon as equity and the safety of the state will admit. Therefore, no article shall be inserted in our constitution, which, either expressly, or by implication may warrant the enacting of laws continuing so impolitic a nuisance."[11] Interest in gradual emancipation was so strong that on May 23 the *Kentucky Gazette* published the New York law on that subject. New York had decided to free any child born after July 4, 1799, but to allow a male born after that date to be held as a servant until the age of twenty-eight and a female until twenty-five.

Few proponents of slavery defended it as an unqualified good. In defending his views George Nicholas admitted, "I never did approve of slavery, but I have thought that the removing of it in a proper manner, would be attended with great difficulties. . . . I will never voluntarily consent to place the business on such footing as will put in the power of one part of the community to be generous at the expense of the other part. . . ." Individual masters, he pointed out, could free their slaves at any time.[12] Most defenders argued that the cost of freeing the slaves was more than either the owners or the state could assume. They also insisted that the slave was not prepared to accept a place in society as a free person.

The 1799 defeat had a dampening effect upon the antislavery forces, although they did not abandon the field. Their continuing efforts took several forms. Year after year they introduced bills calling for yet another convention. While such proposals occasionally passed the house, they died in the senate; proslavery advocates had no desire to subject their peculiar institution to frequent scrutiny. Laws were also sought that would prepare the state and the slaves for the day when a program for general emancipation might at last be passed. These proposals would have curbed the importation of slaves, improved their condition, provided for education, and made individual emancipation easier to accomplish.

The churches that had contributed so much to the early antislavery movements relaxed their opposition. The Methodist General Conferences whittled away on the church's antislavery stance in an effort to placate southern members until little remained except a pious declaration against slavery which many slaveholders could accept. The Presbyterians adopted much the same attitude, although they did call for more education for the Negro. By 1826 fifteen Presbyterian schools for blacks were reported in the state.[13]

Most Baptist churches and associations also moved toward neutrality regarding slavery. In 1805 the Elkhorn Association agreed that it was "improper for ministers, churches or Associations to meddle with emancipation from slavery, or any other political subject; and . . . we advise ministers and churches to have nothing to do therewith in their religious capacities."[14] But some individuals and some churches did not heed such admonitions. One of the prominent dissenters was David Barrow, a Virginian who moved to Montgomery County in 1798. Soon one of the outstanding Baptist preachers in the state, he occupied in the first two decades of the nineteenth century the leading antislavery role that David Rice had assumed earlier.

An earlier move to expel him failed, but at the October 1806 meeting of the North District Association Barrow was charged with "preaching the doctrines of emancipation to the hurt and injury of the brotherhood." When he refused to recant, he was expelled from the association and a committee was appointed to bring his case before the Mount Sterling Church where he held membership. Three churches then withdrew from the association in protest, and two ministers resigned. In 1807 the association revoked its action, but the seceders refused to return and they were soon joined by others who shared their views on emancipation. Led by Barrow and Carter Tarrant and supported by James Garrard, recent governor of the state, they formed their own organization among the dissenting churches in the northcentral part of the state. A preliminary meeting was held in August 1807; the following month they organized the Baptized Licking-Locust Association, Friends of Humanity.

The new association defined its views on slavery after careful consideration of eleven questions relating to that institution. Anyone "whose practice appears friendly to perpetual slavery" was to be excluded, with exceptions for such cases as a woman whose husband opposed emancipation or a person whose slave could not support himself if freed. No member was to buy slaves except to free them, and even then he should have prior approval of his church. A contemporary Baptist writer placed the strength of the new association at twelve' churches and 300 members, but it dissolved after David Barrow's death in 1819.[15]

Some opponents of slavery who were not convinced that a church was the best vehicle for expressing their views formed the Kentucky Abolition Society in 1808. The society probably never had over 200 members, but for some fifteen years it was Kentucky's most important antislavery organization. David Barrow, its president for several years, contributed much to the limited success of the society. In its first meeting in 1808 the group adopted a constitution that declared, "Slavery is a system of oppression pregnant with moral, national and domestic evils, ruinous to national tranquility, honor and enjoyment, and which every good man wishes to be abolished, could such abolition take place upon a plan which would be honorable to the state, safe to the citizen and salutary to the slaves." Members pledged themselves to work for the constitutional abolition of slavery, for the education of free blacks, for better treatment of slaves until they were freed, for the freeing of persons held illegally in bondage, and for the end of the slave trade. Local chapters were to be formed wherever possible, with annual state meetings to coordinate local efforts. Petitions and memorials were viewed as a major weapon, and plans were made to publish materials that would convince slaveholders of their wrongdoing. While Baptists constituted the largest element in the society, members of several other denominations also joined.

The society's most important publication was Barrow's fifty-page pamphlet, *Involuntary, Unmerited, Perpetual, Absolute, Hereditary Slavery Examined on the Principles of Nature, Reason, Justice, Policy and Scripture*, published in 1808. He chided slaveholders for their reluctance to employ the word "slave"; they knew that it was "very odious to all true republicans and lovers of the rights of man. . . ." Open your eyes, he commanded his readers: "He who will enslave a black now . . . would not spare you, if he had you legally in his power." Barrow refused to waste time in argument over slavery in ancient days; the question to be discussed was whether slavery could be justified by any of the principles listed in his title. He had his answer: "I said it cannot. . . ." He argued that the biblical defense was not valid, since slavery in 1808 was not what was meant by slavery in the Bible. Barrow was impressed by what slaves had accomplished within the restrictions placed upon them; he rejected the belief in the innate inferiority of blacks that was accepted even by most antislavery whites. "Indeed I believe I may venture to say, their talents or natural abilities, are not inferior to the whites in any respect; and evidences are not wanting to prove, where opportunity has been afforded them, that they are equal to any other people in arts, etc." Barrow was not concerned that freedom for the blacks would lead to intermarriage with whites. "It has long been my sentiment," he wrote, "that any woman who is good enough to make a man a concubine, etc. ought to serve him for a wife."[16]

In an effort to reach a wider audience, the Kentucky Abolition Society decided in 1821 to publish a newspaper, for some state papers were refusing to accept articles and letters expressing antislavery views. The Reverend John Finley Crowe agreed to edit the paper in Shelbyville. A lack of subscribers caused the proposed semimonthly to be changed to a monthly before the first issue of the sixteen-page *Abolition Intelligencer and Missionary Magazine* appeared in May 1822.

This and Benjamin Lundy's *Genius of Universal Emancipation* were the only two antislavery publications in the nation. The subscription list never exceeded 500, and after twelve issues publication ceased. During its brief lifetime its firm opposition to slavery attracted adverse attention and Crowe received numerous threats.

When Benjamin Lundy attempted to count the nation's "abolition" societies in 1827, he listed 24 in the free states with 1,500 members and 106 with 5,125 members in the slave states. Kentucky had 8 societies with 200 members. These groups were not abolitionist as the term would be used within the next few years; they advocated gradual, constitutional emancipation, perhaps with compensation. While they did not accomplish their goals, they kept the antislavery issue alive and under discussion. In this they were aided by the national controversy over the admission of Missouri into the Union as a slave state. When an effort was made to block admission, the resulting controversy and ultimate compromise focused attention on slavery, and particularly the expansion of slavery, as nothing else had done during the young nation's history. If the dispute alarmed aging Thomas Jefferson "like a firebell ringing in the night," the tolling of the bell disturbed many Kentuckians as well.

A major problem encountered by the emancipationists was the widely held belief that the Negro was not prepared for freedom and that free blacks formed a dangerous element in the community. "A Voter in Fayette" admitted that the institution of slavery itself was largely responsible for that situation. Slaves had "no inducement to acts of virtue; as they never can arrive at respectability. Consequently they are stupid, lazy and void of honesty. Then if liberated they would find it impossible to correct their long established habits of vice. . . ."[17] Most Kentuckians were not willing to accept emancipation if it increased the small number of free blacks in the state. The presence of free blacks was held to make slaves discontented with their status and to increase the danger of runaways and revolts. Henry Clay expressed the sentiments of many Kentuckians when he asserted in 1829 that "the free people of color are, by far as a class, the most corrupt, depraved and abandoned. . . . They are not slaves, and yet they are not free. . . . prejudices, more powerful than any law, deny them the privileges of freedom. They occupy a middle station between the free white population and the slaves of the United States, and the tendency of their habits is to corrupt both."[18] Although the free blacks in Kentucky never numbered more than one percent of the population, the fear was that emancipation would swell their number.

To alleviate this fear, most Kentucky opponents of slavery during the early nineteenth century turned their attention to colonization. They knew, of course, that colonization alone would not free any slaves, but by providing a means of removing freedmen from the state they hoped to encourage both voluntary emancipation and the adoption of some more comprehensive scheme.

The American Colonization Society for the Free People of Color was organized in Washington, D.C., during the winter of 1816–1817. Its avowed purpose was "the removal to the Coast of Africa, with their own consent, of such people of colour within the United States, as are already free, and of such others as the humanity of individuals, and the laws of the different states, may hereafter liberate." Henry Clay, long active in the movement, acknowledged the hope that a successful program would advance the cause of emancipation, but he emphatically denied any intention "of interfering, in the smallest degree, with the rights of property, or the object of emancipation, gradual or immediate."[19] Such disclaimers permitted slaveholders, including Clay, to play important roles in the Colonization Society while remaining aloof from abolitionist groups. Some staunch defenders of slavery suspected that the society was a disguised abolitionist agency, and some determined opponents of slavery described its efforts as too ineffective to merit support. An embarrassingly high percentage of free blacks indicated strong aversion to Liberia. This was not surprising, for some blacks who lived in the United States in the 1820s represented the fifth and sixth generations of their families in America.

Kentucky got its first auxiliary colonization society in 1823 and its second in 1827. The antislavery societies were gradually absorbed into the new movement or died out. Several churches endorsed the plan, as did a number of newspapers, and colonization soon acquired an aura of respectability. Resolutions were introduced frequently in the legislature to secure approval and possible support. A select senate committee was convinced in early 1827 that "such a removal is practicable, and would be highly beneficial, both to the subjects of it and to ourselves. . . . That it could tend to mitigate the evils of slavery, and offer facilities and inducements to voluntary emancipation, seems almost certain; and it cannot be doubted but that this may be done without impairing the rights of property or the safety of society."[20]

In 1829 the Kentucky Colonization Society was organized as a state auxiliary of the national body. The next year four field agents began recruiting members and helping establish local societies. By 1832 Kentucky had at least thirty-one colonization societies, a figure exceeded only by Virginia (thirty-four) and Ohio (thirty-three). Between them, Virginia and Kentucky had nearly 45 percent of the colonization societies in the slave states.[21]

The Danville society, founded in 1829, was probably typical of the state's more active groups. Dues were a dollar per year, or ten dollars for a life membership, and special campaigns raised funds for specific purposes. Danville clergymen were asked to take up collections to promote the cause, and the society sought state appropriations to expand the project. Contributions were made to the state organization. Five vice-presidents assisted President Joshua Fry in carrying out the society's program. By 1830 the board of managers was seeking one or more free blacks to undertake the move to Liberia. The board offered to assist any slaveholder who wanted to free slaves for colonization; at the master's request the board would hire out a slave until the cost of his passage (estimated at twenty to thirty-five dollars) had been earned. By the mid-1830s the Danville society, including women as well as men, had seventy-one members.

At its May 15, 1835 meeting the society passed resolutions to clarify its stand on slavery. One resolution repudiated the type of abolitionism that William Lloyd Garrison had made infamous in recent years: "That abolitionism and especially the spirit of modern abolition, will rather retard than promote the cause of emancipation." But the society condemned the institution of slavery "as a great moral and political evil, opposed to the Spirit of Christianity and of our free institutions." The members denied that their organization had produced "a malignant and persecuting spirit" against free blacks as some uninformed critics had claimed.[22]

Henry Clay was a consistent supporter of colonization for over thirty years although he owned thirty-three slaves the year before his death. Throughout his association with the society, including his term as president, Clay insisted that the organization's concern was with colonizing free blacks, not in the freeing of slaves. "Our object," he emphasized in a major address in 1827, "has been to point out the way, to show that colonization is practicable, and to leave it to those States or individuals, who may be pleased to engage in the object, to prosecute it." While he admitted that not all blacks could be sent to Africa, Clay argued that the program could reduce the black element in the population and thus attain "the desirable objects of domestic tranquility, and render us one homogeneous people." The annual increase of slaves in the South was 46,000, Clay explained, while the free blacks in the nation were increasing by 6,000 each year. The total increase could be sent to Africa each year for only $1,040,000 if masters freed their slaves. "There is a moral fitness," he declared, "in the idea of returning to Africa her children, whose ancestors have been torn from her by the ruthless hand of fraud and violence."

Lest he be misunderstood, Clay repeated that the American Colonization Society "neither has the power nor the will to affect the property of any one contrary to his consent. . . . The Society, composed of free men, concerns itself only with the free." After the early 1830s Henry Clay was much concerned by the pernicious effect that he believed the rise of abolition was having on the general welfare of the slaves and on the success of the colonization movement.[23]

Despite all arguments to the contrary, Clay remained convinced that colonization would work and must work to avoid the possibility of future slave revolts. The blacks were "rational beings, like ourselves, capable of feeling, of reflection, and of judging of what naturally belongs to them as a portion of the human race. By the very conditions of the relation which subsists between us, we are enemies of each other." When the state society purchased the 40-mile-square "Kentucky in Liberia" from the American Colonization Society in 1845, its capital was named "Clay Ashland" in honor of the most prominent Kentuckian who supported the concept of colonization.[24]

Joseph R. Underwood, an important Bowling Green politician, was another slaveholder who was a strong supporter of the program. His 1835 address to the Kentucky Colonization Society attracted wide attention when he declared that the colonists in Liberia had made more progress than had the English settlers at Jamestown in the same length of time. He defended the society from pro- and antislavery attacks; its goal was neither to interfere with slavery nor to strengthen it. While slavery was a great evil, Kentuckians could not "consider ourselves accountable for the origin of the evil, nor do we feel bound to adopt every suggestion of intemperate zeal proposing a remedy. The remedy of the abolitionist is not ours. . . . their zeal has overcome their judgment."

In a careful analysis of the practicality of the project, Underwood proposed that colonization should be denied the young and the old. He hoped to send 4,000 blacks to Liberia each year—half of them females aged sixteen and seventeen, the other half males between twenty and twenty-five. If the cost averaged thirty-five dollars per person, the annual expense would be only $140,000; that sum could be raised easily by hiring out a slave for a year prior to his departure. The departure of a large number of women just entering their childbearing years would result in a sharp decline in the growth of the slave population, Underwood argued, and over a period of perhaps fifty years, Kentucky could rid herself of slavery. This was desirable, he insisted, because slave labor was more expensive than free, and free states were outgaining the slave states. Already Kentucky was losing valuable citizens who would not live in a slave environment. He also denounced slavery as a violation of both Christian and democratic doctrines, but his major appeal was to the economic well-being of his fellow citizens.[25]

Underwood's scheme for gradual emancipation was actually at variance with the stated purpose of the society, but many Kentucky supporters of colonization agreed with him. He was disturbed because so few free blacks volunteered to participate in the program, but he was convinced that "slavery cannot continue to exist in this country no matter how dreadful the consequences of abolishing it. . . . I think my remedy would leave the fewest scars behind." Underwood served for several years as a director of the national organization, and in 1842 he chaired a Washington convention that tried to secure federal assistance.[26]

Opposition to colonization came from diametrically opposed groups. Abolitionists saw it as a palliative that might retard their crusade against slavery; Garrison castigated the society severely in an 1832 pamphlet and in the *Liberator*. On the other hand, some slaveholders were never convinced that the secret purpose of the society was not the termination of slavery. Robert Wickliffe, Sr., a prominent slaveholder who belonged to the Kentucky Colonization Society, asserted in a public address that the only purpose was to remove free Negroes from the state. Robert J. Breckinridge and others present disagreed quickly and sharply. Breckinridge announced that if freedom was not the ultimate goal he would wash his hands of the work. Seeing that the majority disagreed with him, Wickliffe withdrew from the organization.[27]

The success of the Colonization Society depended upon the number of slaves it might encourage masters to free and the number of freedmen that could be sent to Liberia. Its record was not good. Difficulties in raising money were chronic; they would have been more serious had many blacks indicated a willingness to make the long voyage. Despite the restrictions under which they lived, most free blacks preferred to remain in the United States. As Frederick Douglass said, "We have grown up in this republic and I see nothing in her character or find in the character of the American people as yet, which compels the belief that we must leave the United States." But the society's members were persistent, funds slowly accumulated, and some ex-slaves agreed to make the trip.

Richard Bibb of Logan County freed fifty-one slaves, thirty-two of whom consented to go to Liberia. Other recruits were found, and on March 22, 1833, a group of Kentucky colonists left Louisville for New Orleans. The society's agent chartered the brig *Ajax* for $3,625, and on April 20 the ship sailed with ninety-nine Kentucky blacks and fifty-one from Tennessee. Unfortunately, cholera and other ailments killed five adults and twenty-four children and forced the ship to put in at Key West. A year later David Richardson wrote Lexington friends that he liked Liberia and was prospering on a ten-acre farm where he raised corn, potatoes, cassava, plantains, and bananas. Only industry was required to make a good living, he said, but prices were so high that immigrants should bring all needed supplies with them.[28]

This initial effort exhausted the funds so laboriously raised. No one was transported from Kentucky between 1834 and 1839, and only a dozen made the voyage in 1840. Agitation for the establishment of "Kentucky in Liberia" brought renewed interest, and more intensive efforts were made to induce free blacks to migrate. Those unable to pay their way were promised passage and support for six months after arrival, and each single adult or head of family was assured of a lot in Clay Ashland and a farm ranging from five to one hundred acres, depending upon the distance from town. In late 1845 the *Rothschild* was chartered to carry 200 Kentucky emigrants to their new home, but when the ship sailed in January 1846 only thirty-four Kentuckians were aboard. Although they were greeted by Governor Joseph J. Roberts when the ship docked on March 15, two of the blacks refused even to go ashore.[29]

Others became discouraged and returned to the United States, for life in Liberia proved more difficult than most had expected, and relations with the natives were not always good. In March 1846 Moses Jackson wrote friends in Jessamine County, "The present state of affairs here is not very flattering, and the people here from all I have seen and heard, take but little interest in the improvement of the country." After commenting upon such attractions as giant snakes, he added, "Tell Absolom Woodfork that I cannot as a friend recommend him to come out here until I have seen more of this place." When Joseph Underwood wrote his wife from Washington on December 15, 1851, he enclosed a letter from Sally, a former slave. "I feel sorry for the poor creature," the senator confessed. "I have no doubt she has often thought of the comforts & happiness she enjoyed when I had to provide for her food & raiment, & I very well understand why she should sigh for what she calls the flesh pots of Egypt. I did not suppose that she would ever be reduced to eating sweet potato tops & crawfish & to talk of snakes & monkeys as delicacies, & to complain that she only got meat once a month. These things are incident to settling in a new country & they will get over it after a while. I will send them some flour & other articles. Her letter will not do much good for the cause of colonization." [30]

Other former slaves adjusted better and were willing to put up with poor conditions in Liberia for the sake of freedom. Nelson Sanders, freed in 1845 by his master's will, reached Liberia in 1846. Two years later he wrote his former mistress, "Liberia is unquestionably the happyest territory for the black man that could be selected on the globe, we enjoy liberty & our lives in a degree which is impossible for the negro to enjoy in any other country. Here is the place whence the Man of Colour, especially a black colour, originated, here it should terminate if possible. . . ." He resented the lies that some people had told in giving "woeful accounts of Liberia . . . it is entirely wrong." [31]

Despite such endorsements and the faithful labors of workers for the movement, the Kentucky Colonization Society never attained great success. The legislature provided some assistance in 1851 by enacting a law that required emancipated slaves to leave the state and prohibited free blacks in other states from entering Kentucky. As a consequence of such restrictions, the free blacks in the state only increased from 10,011 in 1850 to 10,684 a decade later. In 1856 the legislature appropriated $5,000 annually to assist the society in its program. The last sizable party of Kentucky blacks to go to Liberia left in 1857, when forty-two made the journey. The Pleasant Hill Shaker journal entry for May 10 contained a note about the major portion of this group: "Leaving for Liberia Africa 34 of Col. Wm. Thompsons Negroes having been liberated some 2 months ago upon the condition of their going to Liberia passed through this place today at 8½ o'clock enroute to Liberia via Lex. Cinn. Baltimore etc."[32] During the period 1829–1859 the state society sent only 658 emigrants to Africa, a number that had little impact upon the number of slaves within the state. Most Kentuckians who wished to bring an end to slavery turned to other means.

It says something about Kentucky stubbornness to note that in 1866 the state senate passed resolutions requesting the federal government to set aside some area, outside existing states, where blacks could be colonized.

3

THE PIVOTAL YEARS

THE COLONIZATION MOVEMENT was so innocuous and subject to such different interpretations that it could harbor individuals with quite varied opinions of slavery. Many Kentuckians of that era shared a sort of comfortable uneasiness about the institution of slavery. It was an evil, of course, and it would have been well if it had never been introduced into the commonwealth. But realities had to be faced. Slavery was well established, and it was an important aspect of the state's economy. Besides, Kentucky slaves were thought to lead a better life than those in any other state, and with their handicaps slaves were probably better off in bondage than if freed. While they were obviously human, they were not thought capable of enjoying the social and political freedoms of whites. The issue of freedom might have to be faced sometime, but not in the foreseeable future.

Colonization was a moderate movement that alienated both the strong proponents and the determined opponents of slavery. The Missouri controversy focused attention on slavery and enchanced the South's sense of sectional consciousness. During the following years many southerners became convinced that their economic future lay primarily in the production of a few great staple crops that could be grown most profitably on a large scale with the use of slave labor. Kentucky had little to do with the crowning of King Cotton, but such economic changes improved the market for the state's surplus slaves.

Garrison's 1831 publication of the *Liberator* signaled the emergence of a much harsher attack upon slavery and slaveholders. Garrison was never as influential in the antislavery movement as he thought he was, but to many southerners he personified the new abolition, a term that began to mean something quite different from emancipation. Kentuckians who had never owned a slave joined their slaveholding neighbors in resenting the vitriolic attacks that Garrison and others poured forth in their papers and speeches. Warned by John C. Calhoun that the South's position was a minority one and that the region would have to present a united front to its enemies, southerners became less tolerant of dissent and dissenters. Only ten years after Benjamin Lundy found more antislavery societies in the South than in the North, not a single one existed below the Mason-Dixon line.

States' rights also were an important concern of many Kentuckians and had a bearing upon the slavery issue. If a state was actually sovereign, then it could legally nullify an act of Congress or secede from the Union. States' rights have traditionally been used by a minority to check the will of the majority, and as the South became increasingly conscious of itself as a minority, southerners placed more and more emphasis on that doctrine. Most Kentuckians viewed slavery as a state matter that was beyond the jurisdiction of the federal government; what happened to slavery in Kentucky was for Kentuckians to decide. During the pivotal years between 1830 and 1850 Kentuckians made their decision about the peculiar institution and its future.

The career of James G. Birney illustrates the changing attitudes of some citizens. Birney was born in Danville on February 4, 1792. His father, a well-to-do merchant, owned some twenty well-treated slaves, and Birney was reared in a slavery environment. But his father and grandfather had supported Rice in 1792, and the minister was a frequent visitor in their homes. Young Birney was thus exposed to antislavery views at an early age. He may have received additional antislavery tutelage during his two years at Princeton College and the subsequent four years spent studying law in Philadelphia. Birney returned to Danville in 1814 and began to practice his profession. When he married Agatha McDowell in 1816, the young couple received several slaves as wedding gifts.

Few Kentucky lawyers have remained immune from politics, and Birney was elected to the state house of representatives in 1816. On a slavery matter, he opposed a resolution that would have the governor consult with his Indiana and Ohio counterparts in an effort to secure a better return of fugitive slaves. Birney's objection was that no gentleman would lower himself to be a slave catcher, and it was undignified for the state to enter upon that sordid business.

In 1818 Birney moved to a plantation near Huntsville, Alabama, in search of better economic opportunities as a cotton planter. His crops were slave-produced, and Birney's opposition to slavery was confined to fringe reforms—no further importation of slaves into the state, the end of public sales, more certain punishment for cruel masters. Birney had poor crops in the years 1820–1822, and his lavish style of living and lack of gambling skills put him in serious financial condition. He sold his plantation and field slaves in 1823 and moved into Huntsville, where careful attention to his legal practice soon improved his financial position.

Birney became interested in the American Colonization Society about 1826, and he began raising funds for its work. In 1827 he lobbied successfully for an Alabama law that prohibited the importation of slaves for sale or hire; he was greatly disappointed when the act was repealed in 1829. During a visit in 1827 Birney persuaded his Masonic lodge in Danville to protest the importation of slaves into Kentucky. In 1830 when he visited the North to recruit teachers for two schools in which he was interested, Birney was much impressed by the superior conditions he saw there. The disparity, he decided, was due to slavery in the South.

His growing distress over slavery gradually led Birney to the conclusion that colonization did not provide a satisfactory answer. He also decided that as soon as possible he would move to a free state. "I shall not live a legal slave-holder any longer than till I can devise the wisest and safest way of putting my slaves into legal possession of themselves, and making such provisions for them in liberty as justice and benevolence require," he told Theodore D. Weld when the latter visited Alabama in 1832.[1] Their conversations helped solidify Birney's antislavery sentiments.

Despite his growing doubts about the effectiveness of colonization, during the summer of 1832 Birney accepted the position of agent for the national society in a five-state area. He sought to convince southerners that colonization was not a northern plot, and in August 1833 he began publishing articles advocating gradual emancipation and colonization in the *Huntsville Democrat*. In a September letter he recorded his thoughts about the near future. "What I would now suggest would be *to press with every energy upon Maryland, Virginia, and Kentucky for emancipation and colonization*. If one of those States be not detached from the number of slaveholding States, *the slave question must inevitably dissolve the Union*, and that before very long. Should Virginia (or Maryland or Kentucky) leave them, the Union will be safe, though the sufferings of the South will be almost unto death. Indeed, I am by no means certain but that Lower Mississippi and the country bordering on the Gulf of Mexico will ultimately be peopled almost entirely by blacks."[2]

Finally disenchanted with colonization, Birney resigned his position and in November 1833 moved back to Kentucky and bought a farm near Danville. "I looked upon it as the *best site in our whole country for taking a stand against slavery*," he wrote Gerrit Smith.[3] He helped organize a Lexington society for the purpose of freeing future children of slaves at some agreed date. Such a society had been formed in 1831–1832, but had languished. Birney's attempt to revive it had at first disappointing results. Some original members had since changed their minds, while others judged the time inopportune; the Nat Turner revolt in Virginia in 1831 had been a severe blow to antislavery groups. Only nine persons attended the first meeting, but Birney insisted that a start be made, and they formed "The Kentucky Society for the Gradual Relief of the State from Slavery," independent of the colonization movement. Members pledged themselves to free at age twenty-five all slaves born in the future as their property. Children of such slaves would become free with their mothers. Birney insisted that membership be open to all adult white citizens of Kentucky, and a number of women joined. By the close of 1834 the society had sixty to seventy members.[4]

While the society's constitution admitted that the "emancipation of the present generation of slaves among us" was probably impossible, the ultimate goal was "the total abolition of slavery throughout the Commonwealth." Meanwhile, they proposed "*immediate* preparation for *future* emancipation." The first step was to decide "*that slavery shall cease to exist —absolutely, unconditionally and irrevocably.*" Then plans could be made for its termination. While the society's constitution did not deal with the status of freed blacks, the "Address" urged preparatory education, including apprenticeships, and encouraged voluntary migration to Africa. Arguments over the status of free blacks should not obstruct a systematic scheme of gradual emancipation.[5]

Similar organizations were formed in other parts of the state, although the goal of one in each county was not met. While most members were slaveholders, defenders of slavery were suspicious of them. Opinions on antislavery were hardening, and some people who were at least moderately antislavery were no longer willing to be associated openly with the antislavery cause. The small membership of the groups was not a true indication of the antislavery sentiment in Kentucky.

The development of the abolitionist crusade against slavery in the 1830s finally convinced Birney that gradual emancipation was not enough. He was much impressed by Lane Seminary's great slavery debate in 1834, and he corresponded extensively with a number of leading abolitionists. By 1835 he was converted to their views. He despaired of receiving substantial help from Kentucky slaveholders, who would admit the truth of antislavery arguments but then reject the logical solution. If a gradual emancipation law ever passed, they would sell most of their slaves to the Lower South. Birney emancipated six slaves that he still owned in 1834, paying the husband wages he would have received had he been free and hiring the family as free workers. Later, when he left the state, Birney found jobs for the family and made provisions for educating a mulatto girl who was not a member of the family. Few Kentuckians followed his example.

In 1834 Birney resigned as vice-president of the Kentucky Colonization Society and published a *Letter on Colonization* declaring that this program could not accomplish its aims. The letter attracted wide attention and established Birney's reputation among the abolitionists. It also aroused increased opposition in Kentucky, and he confessed, "I do not believe I can remain in Kentucky. . . ." But "To remove now would look like surrendering the cause in Kentucky without having made any effort for success and taking refuge, as it were, among strangers," and Birney still hoped to attract enough support to justify continuing the struggle in his native state.

When Birney and Dr. John C. Young, president of Centre College, debated slavery before the school's literary societies the young men rejected abolition by a narrow 22-to-20 margin. The state's youths were being corrupted, and Birney was "much vilified and abused about Danville. . . ." His immediate hope was to win converts by publishing an antislavery newspaper in Danville, and he toured much of the state in the early fall of 1834 in an effort to enlist the aid of as many Presbyterian ministers as possible. During his tour Birney also visited Henry Clay at Ashland, but the politician rejected Birney's arguments. They continued to correspond, but Birney concluded that "Mr. Clay had no *conscience* about this matter, and therefore . . . would swim with the popular current."[6]

Birney's synod denounced slavery and called for gradual, voluntary emancipation by a vote of 56 to 8 with 7 members abstaining. Encouraged by this token, Birney moved in 1835 to form the Kentucky Anti-Slavery Society and to affiliate with the American Anti-Slavery Society organized two years earlier. This was an important change, for Birney had previously remained aloof from direct association with northern abolitionist groups. The Kentucky society had some forty members, but Birney noted the absence of the slaveholders who had constituted much of the influential membership of the colonization societies. "Immediate emancipation will have to be sustained here by the comparatively poor and humble," he wrote Gerrit Smith.[7]

Birney was well received in the North during a spring and summer tour in 1835. His role as an abolitionist in a slave state and his former ownership of slaves attracted attention, and his speaking ability and gracious platform appearance captivated those who heard him. He preached that slavery had to be abolished to preserve the Union. Not as rash as some of his new associates, the Kentuckian urged immediate action to stop the interstate slave trade and to abolish slavery in the District of Columbia and the territories.

Birney planned to begin publication of the *Philanthropist* in Danville on August 1, and as that date approached, Kentucky reaction became more agitated. Thirty citizens remonstrated on July 12 against "the peril that must and inevitably will attend the execution of your paper." They asked him to suspend publication until the legislature had time to act on the question. In moderate tones, they warned him to "beware how you make an experiment here, which no *American Slave-holding Community* had found itself able to bear."[8] Birney rejected their appeal as a violation of the constitutional right to a free press; there was no way to curb the discussion already under way.

Several hundred persons who attended a public meeting in the Danville Baptist Church on July 25 adopted resolutions that denounced the intended newspaper as "a direct attack upon, and a wanton disregard of our domestic relations." A committee of five was appointed to urge Birney to give up the undertaking.[9] Birney continued with his plans for publication, but they were soon thwarted. S. S. Dismukes, publisher of Danville's *Olive Branch*, was to print the paper, but he succumbed to pressure and suddenly decided to move to Missouri. Birney was then unable to secure another printer.

He also encountered difficulty in finding halls in which to speak, and he suspected that his mail was being tampered with. To struggle longer seemed hopeless, and on September 13, 1835, he wrote Gerrit Smith, "I begin to think, it is time for Christians to leave the slaveholding States. . . . There will be no cessation of the strife, until Slavery shall be exterminated, or liberty destroyed."[10]

George Prentice, editor of the *Louisville Journal*, wrote that Birney, unlike Garrison, "has the courage to reside among the people whose institutions he assails." Birney did not slink away. He sold his farm, tidied up his affairs, and purchased a house in Cincinnati before making the move. He continued his antislavery activities in the North, but his departure was a severe blow to the state's antislavery movement, and the Kentucky Anti-Slavery Society soon waned. When his father died in 1839 Birney requested that the twenty slaves be included in his share of the estate. Then he freed them and made careful provision for their welfare.[11]

While Birney's efforts did not pose a serious threat to slavery in Kentucky, the rise of the abolitionist movement in the North alarmed many of the state's slaveholders, who adopted a more aggressive defense of their institution. Yet during the early 1830s there was a demand for another constitutional convention that would provide for some plan of gradual emancipation. Birney wrote Lewis Tappan on February 3, 1833, "Emancipation in some form or another occupies the minds of the community, and . . . the feeling in favor of it is growing." The first formal step toward a convention came in 1837 when the senate (20–16) and house (57–42) gave approval.

But the proposal had to be approved by the voters in two general elections before the General Assembly could issue the call. Interest was widespread across the nation, for it was assumed that Kentucky's action would influence other slave states outside the Lower South. The *Genius of Universal Emancipation* declared that "Kentucky is now the battleground of abolition."[12] Kentucky emancipationists denied repeatedly any connection with northern abolitionists, but the voters apparently thought otherwise. Henry Clay wrote Birney, whom he still respected: "Will you believe me, when I assure you that it is my clear conviction that the decision against a Convention was mainly produced by the agitation of the question of abolition at the North? I will not say that, without that agitation, the State was ripe for gradual emancipation, but it was rapidly advancing to that point. We are thrown back fifty years."[13]

The vote against the convention was nearly four to one. Resentment against abolitionist attacks undoubtedly contributed to the outcome, as did the growing belief that the slave states could protect themselves only by presenting a united front against the enemy. The problem of fugitive slaves irked many Kentuckians and increased their resistance to northern demands. Some emancipationists, most notably Robert J. Breckinridge, also contended that the 1799 constitution, if properly interpreted, provided adequate means of securing emancipation.

During the early 1830s Kentuckians had devoted considerable attention to the importation of slaves into the state. The legislature had passed an anti-importation law in 1794, and the 1798 slave code prohibited the importation of slaves from foreign countries or those who had come to the United States from a foreign country after 1789. Section 26 of the code imposed a $300 fine for each slave imported as merchandise, but a citizen could bring in slaves for his own use if they had not entered the country since 1789, and immigrants to Kentucky from other states could bring their slaves with them. Acts of 1814 and 1815 made minor modifications, the most important being an oath that an immigrant was to deposit with the county clerk within 60 days of his arrival: "I,———, do swear that my removal to the state of Kentucky was with the intention of becoming a citizen thereof, and that I have brought no slave or slaves to this state, with the intention of selling them."[14]

The law could not be effectively enforced, and its notorious evasions and the rapid growth of the slave population led to increased demands for more effective legislation. Some advocates of colonization and voluntary emancipation saw in nonimportation a means of slowing the growth of the slave population and thereby increasing the possibility of attaining their goals. Some slaveholders saw in nonimportation a means of increasing the value of their slaves.[15] In the late 1820s and early 1830s the legislature received numerous petitions demanding an improved law.

When such a bill was introduced in the senate, some supporters argued that gradual emancipation was inevitable and could be accomplished more easily if the number of slaves was curbed. This argument was accepted by *Niles' Weekly Register* in the February 6, 1830 issue: "That slavery had been highly injurious to Kentucky is undoubted; and that measures will be taken to rid the state of its slave population, so far as may be consistent with what are esteemed the rights of property, is entirely manifest to us. The first step toward that is an absolute prohibition of their importation from other states." Opponents of the measure charged that it was unconstitutional and that it would force other states to prohibit Kentucky products. While the vote was often close, supporters of the bill did not secure passage until February 1833.

The act provided that anyone who imported slaves himself, or knowingly bought, sold, or hired imported slaves, should be fined $600 per slave involved. Bona fide immigrants could bring with them slaves for their own use, but within sixty days of arrival the owner had to swear that he had no intention of selling them. A Kentucky citizen who inherited out-of-state slaves or received them as a marriage gift was allowed to import them.[16] County attorneys were sworn to enforce the law; their diligence in doing so was encouraged by a fee that was 20 percent of the sum collected.

It is difficult to assess the effects of the act. The percentage of blacks in the population declined after 1830, but other factors, such as the state's economic development, may have been more important than the act. While some slaveholders had approved it as a means of raising the value of their slaves, in time the Act of 1833 came to be interpreted as a move toward ending slavery, and as such it became a focal point for the slavery controversy within the state. No other Kentucky slavery statute caused as much controversy as this one.

The proslavery element made frequent efforts to secure the act's repeal, with "Old Duke" Robert Wickliffe one of the leaders in such efforts. Senate approval was occasionally secured, but the house consistently rejected repeal. A concession was made in 1841 when the penalty was waived for any immigrant who, within six months, swore that he was ignorant of the oath required by the Act of 1833. A similar profession of ignorance also protected anyone who had purchased illegal slaves prior to passage of the 1841 law.[17] Such waivers were common during the 1840s.

The continuing debates over slavery did much to enliven Kentucky's political affairs. Politicians were frequently questioned on their attitude toward the 1833 law, and their answers often determined their success with the voters. During the late 1830s and early 1840s a new antislavery leader appeared on the political scene who was destined to become one of the most exciting and colorful figures in the history of the commonwealth.

Cassius Marcellus Clay was born in Madison County in 1810, the son of General Green Clay, one of the state's wealthiest slaveholders. While at Yale College, Cassius heard Garrison speak on slavery. "This was a new revelation to me," Clay wrote later. "I then resolved . . . that, when I had the strength, if ever, I would give slavery a death struggle."[18] But Clay did not convert instantaneously to antislavery. Elected to the legislature in 1835, Clay condemned the "horde of fanatical incendiaries" in the North. He had once favored gradual emancipation, but "Such considerations, Sir, belong to the past and not to the present. . . . I almost give way to the belief that slavery must continue to exist till, like some uneradicable disease, it disappears with the body that gave it being."[19]

Defeated in 1836, Clay was elected to the house once more in 1837. Of his antislavery views during this period Clay only said, "I began to develop my opposition to slavery," and he was never one to belittle his accomplishments. But by 1840 when he ran again for state representative Clay emerged as a defender of the Act of 1833 and a determined advocate of emancipation. Two Fayette County candidates were almost assured of election; the real contest was between Clay and Robert Wickliffe, Jr., for the third seat. Clay endorsed the Act of 1833 as a means of keeping more slaves out of Fayette County, which already had a surplus. He also introduced the economic argument that became his main theme for the rest of his antislavery career. While he declared in 1840, "I believe *slavery* to be an *evil*—an evil morally, economically, physically, intellectually, socially, religiously, politically . . . an unmixed evil," Cassius Clay never emphasized the moral and religious arguments that Birney had stressed. "It is not a matter of conscience with me," Clay once admitted. "I press it not upon the consciences of others." Instead he emphasized the unhappy economic consequence of slavery upon non-slaveholders. He used statistics extensively to show that Kentucky's economic development lagged far behind that of such free-state neighbors as Ohio.[20]

During the 1840 campaign the Wickliffes charged that Clay was actually an abolitionist, one of the group trying "to get up a war between the slave holders and the non-slave holders" that would end slavery in the state.[21] Despite such charges, Clay won a narrow victory in an exciting race that attracted wide attention. Never again would Cassius Clay win an election to public office.

In the house Clay helped turn back renewed efforts to repeal the Act of 1833. He reiterated his plea to working-class whites to look to their own best interests instead of following the dictates of slaveholders. His failure to arouse them was due to many factors, including dislike and even fear of the abolitionists. Clay, like many later historians, also failed to understand "the southern class system, in which there were no sharp cleavages between slaveowner and nonslaveholder, who were bound together by ties of kinship, friendship, and economic opportunity."[22] In whatever lowly economic status a poor white found himself, he had the psychological assurance that he was superior to all blacks, no matter how much better off they might be in material terms. This racial distinction helped forge a bond between poor whites and wealthy planters that often baffled and infuriated opponents of slavery.

Clay continued his antislavery campaign after his 1841 defeat for reelection, and his well-publicized duels and bloody encounters made him nationally known and obscured the mildness of his views. He insisted that he favored emancipation "not because we love the black man best, for we do not love him as well . . . but because it is just" and because the end of slavery would increase the prosperity of whites and of the state as a whole. In his private letters Clay often dismissed the Negroes as inferior. "They lack self-reliance—we can make nothing out of them," he once wrote. "God has made them for the sun and the banana!"[23]

Time and again Clay denied that he was an abolitionist. Although he occasionally changed details, his goal was gradual emancipation through legal means. For years he sought a convention that would amend the constitution to provide that every female slave born after a designated date (perhaps as early as 1860, perhaps as late as 1900) would become free at twenty-one. Since a child had the status of its mother, slavery would ultimately be terminated. The process would be hastened, Clay asserted, because many masters would sell their slaves out of state to avoid loss.[24]

Clay continued to own slaves until 1844. When he finally decided upon emancipation, he purchased thirteen slaves for $10,000 to keep families intact. A contemporary account estimated his total loss at $40,000, a figure that would indicate the freeing of some fifty persons, but other estimates ran as high as a hundred. Many of the freedmen remained at White Hall as free laborers. Clay retained a number of slaves who belonged to the family estate, not to him personally, and for this, devout abolitionists severely criticized him.

Had he been easily influenced, Clay would never have established an antislavery newspaper in Lexington. But he was having difficulty finding papers that would publish what the editor of the *Lexington Observer* called his "militant and provocative" pieces, and so in January 1845 Clay issued a prospectus for the *True American*, to be devoted to the cause of gradual and constitutional emancipation. The proslavery people considered the proposal a direct challenge to their established order. The *Lexington Observer* warned that Clay had "taken the very worst time," for the abolitionists' crusade "had produced a state of feeling in the minds of slaveholders anything but propitious to the slave or his liberation. . . ." Yet Clay's proposal was so mild that Garrison could not endorse it, although he did agree to collect the $2.50 subscription from northern supporters. Garrison predicted accurately that the paper would not be tolerated unless Clay became an apologist for slavery.[25]

The first issue on June 3 went to 300 in-state and 1,700 out-of-state subscribers. Clay's main appeal was to the economic self-interest of non-slaveholding whites, and he was careful to advocate only constitutional emancipation. But the existence of the paper was an affront to the slaveholding community, and Clay's action in fortifying the paper's building on North Mill Street indicated that he expected trouble. The novice editor received threatening letters ("The hemp is ready for your neck") and on July 16 an *Observer* editorial asked, "Slaveholders of Fayette, is it not now time for you to act on this matter yourselves . . . ?"

The crisis came when Clay was recovering from typhoid fever. The August 12 issue carried an article by an anonymous slaveholder advocating political equality for free blacks and much improved conditions for slaves. Clay compounded the outrage by an accompanying editorial dictated from his sickbed. After yet another plea for emancipation, he concluded with a warning that was interpreted as an appeal to violence and slave lust. "But remember, you who dwell in marble palaces, that there are strong arms and fiery hearts and iron pikes in the streets, and pains [*sic*] of glass only between them and the silver plate on the board and the smooth-skinned woman on the ottoman. When you have mocked at virtue, denied the agency of God in the affairs of men, and made rapine your honeyed faith, tremble! for the day of retribution is at hand, and the masses will be avenged!"

A courthouse meeting of some two dozen citizens on August 14 was interrupted when Clay appeared. So weak that he had to recline on a bench, he denounced the group as consisting largely of Democrats and his personal enemies. He also swore that he was utterly opposed to slave revolts. After his departure the group voted to ask Clay to discontinue publication to preserve the peace and safety of the community. Clay rejected the demand the next day in a handbill extra in which he called upon free laborers to support him. He closed on a note of defiance: "Go tell your secret conclave of cowardly assassins that C. M. Clay knows his rights and how to defend them."

The committee then called a mass public meeting for the courthouse yard on Monday, August 18. In more handbills Clay repeated his views on emancipation, repudiated the offensive article, and admitted that his illness had "almost incessantly" affected his brain. Disclaiming any support from slaves or abolitionists, he added, "I am willing to take warning from friends or enemies for the future conduct of my paper. . . ."[26] That conciliatory gesture came far too late to have any effect.

The large crowd that gathered in the courthouse yard that Monday heard a letter read in which Clay promised to publish nothing "upon this subject for which I am not willing to be held responsible." He announced that the multiple defenses of his office had been dismantled, leaving it defended only by law. Thomas F. Marshall then delivered an able address in which he defended suppression because public safety was the superior law. Clay had become the tool of abolitionists, he said. "Such a man and such a course is no longer tolerable or consistent with the character or safety of this community. . . . the negroes might well, as we have strong reason to believe they do, look to him as a deliverer. . . . A Kentuckian himself, he should have known Kentuckians better."[27]

A Committee of Sixty was appointed to seize the press and ship it to Cincinnati. In the meantime a police court judge issued an injunction suspending publication of the paper and seizing its plant. Clay surrendered his keys to the city marshal, and the removal proceeded smoothly after the Lexington mayor told the committeemen that though their action was illegal, the city could not contest it.

Most Kentuckians approved the action. Clay had failed to

rally significant support on such an issue as freedom of the press. Several of Lexington's free blacks were brutally attacked the day after the mass meeting, and the *Christian Intelligencer*, a small Methodist paper published in Georgetown, was forced to cease publication after the editor condemned the Lexington proceedings. Public meetings endorsed the action taken, and Clay was condemned in numerous newspapers. Many abolitionists faced a dilemma. They wanted to denounce the slavocracy for the action taken, but Clay was not sound enough on the subject of slavery to merit unstinted praise. Garrison's comments were very restrained, although Frederick Douglass wrote from England that the *True American* had been "one of the most hopeful and soul-cheering signs of the times,—a star shining in darkness, beaming hope to the almost despairing bondsman."[28]

Early in October subscribers received the *True American* again. Clay edited it in Lexington and printed it in Cincinnati where the press had been reassembled. But some vital spark was missing, and no issue created the excitement that had followed the August 12 paper. A bill to exclude antislavery publications from the state was defeated in the house in early 1846; it might well have passed in the August excitement. The last issue that Clay edited again contained his denial of any association with the abolitionists. "They have no more right to come here and declaim against slavery," he wrote, "than we have to go to Russia and denounce despotism of the same sort there." Clay was not a good editor, and he became bored with the time-consuming task. He was glad to give it up in May 1846 to ride off to the Mexican War.

John C. Vaughan, a South Carolinian who had lived for some time in Ohio, became editor of the *True American* with Brutus Clay supervising operations as fiscal agent for his brother. When northern support declined sharply in protest of Cassius's participation in the war, Brutus halted publication. Vaughan secured enough backing to establish the *Examiner*, a mild emancipationist paper, in Louisville. From September 11, 1847, to June 10, 1848, it featured a comprehensive series of twenty articles supporting emancipation written by James

Madison Pendleton, an able young Baptist minister. Kentucky lost a valuable opponent of slavery when Pendleton moved to Tennessee in 1857.[29] Vaughan encountered little opposition, but he also received little support, and the *Examiner* died of financial starvation in 1849.

Another doughty supporter of emancipation was the Reverend Robert Jefferson Breckinridge, son of John Breckinridge. This irascible Presbyterian clergyman engaged in many controversies within and without his church, but one of his most bitter and prolonged quarrels was with Robert Wickliffe, Sr., in the 1840s. Their lengthy tirades enriched Bluegrass printers who published pamphlets that were eagerly read across the state. Breckinridge was not always a comfortable ally for other antislavery people, who were disappointed by his refusal to join the fight for a constitutional convention. It was unnecessary, Breckinridge argued as early as 1830; the state had the power to secure emancipation by enacting laws to free the children born of slaves. Breckinridge also favored supporting colonization by a special tax placed on slaves.[30]

James T. Morehead was another longtime advocate of emancipation and colonization. State legislator, governor, United States senator, he was one of the finest speakers in a state noted for its orators. Morehead also opposed the idea of a convention in the late 1830s; his reason was shared by a number of other emancipationists. "Any man who desires to see slavery abolished—any friend of emancipation, gradual or immediate—who supposes for a moment that now is the time to carry out this favorite policy, must be blind to the prognostics that lower from every quarter of the political sky," he declared in 1838. "Four years ago you might have had some hope. But the wild spirit of fanaticism has done much to retard the work of emancipation and to rivet the fetters of slavery in Kentucky."[31]

Such reactions had almost ended the antislavery agitation of the churches by the 1840s. The General Conference of the Methodist Church met in Cincinnati in 1836 and by a wide margin declared that the church would not interfere with the civil and political aspects of slavery. Abolitionism was then denounced overwhelmingly. While some individual Methodists continued their antislavery work, most churches and conferences were increasingly careful to avoid offending either their slaveholding members or the general community. When the Methodist church split over slavery, the 1845 Kentucky conference voted by a decisive margin to join the Methodist Episcopal Church South, and official antislavery agitation almost ceased. Baptist churches also gradually abandoned most of their antislavery activities, and when the Baptists split nationally in 1844–1845 practically all of the Kentucky congregations allied themselves with the southern group.

Such members as Robert Breckinridge did not let the Presbyterian church in Kentucky ignore the slavery question as some members wanted to do. In 1833 the Synod of Kentucky voted 41 to 36 to postpone indefinitely any decision on "the very difficult and delicate question of slavery, as it exists within our bounds. . . ." Whereupon Breckinridge rose from his seat, picked up his hat, and strode from the hall, declaiming on his way: "God has left you, and I also will now leave you, and have no more correspondence with you."[32] But the synod did condemn the institution of slavery, and it established a committee to draft a plan for the education and future emancipation of slaves. The plan, written largely by John C. Young, was published two years later. It called for gradual emancipation with slaves then under twenty years of age, along with those born in the future, to become free at twenty-five. The report placed heavy emphasis upon education to prepare slaves for freedom. But the tide was turning against emancipation, and the synod never acted upon the report. Individuals continued the struggle, and the Presbyterian ministers as a group were probably more antislavery than those of any other major denomination in the state.

As opposition to emancipation increased, the Non-Importation Act of 1833 came under attack until it was finally repealed in 1849. Warner Lewis Underwood wrote about the house debate on the bill in his diary on February 11: "The idea is up in the Legislature that it is popular to be a decided pro-slavery man—and many a little soul hopes to win distinction by trying to be a leader in the new party which may be formed on the negro question." The new law allowed individuals to import slaves for their own use but prohibited their sale for five years.

Their defeat on the Non-Importation Act might have forewarned the antislavery people of the fate that awaited them in the constitutional convention, but a number of Kentuckians were convinced that the time was propitious for establishing a plan for gradual emancipation. Their efforts had lagged after their 1838 defeat, but in 1847 the legislature passed a bill that set the first of two required public votes for August 1847. The 1799 constitution needed revision, and the voters approved the call for a convention. While the antislavery element was active, particularly in Louisville where the growing German population was strongly antislavery, slavery was not the dominant issue in the election. The next election, held in 1848, produced much the same margin, and the legislature provided for the election of 100 delegates on August 8, 1849, with the convention to assemble in Frankfort on October 1. A major campaign to determine the membership then began, and, while other subjects were discussed, slavery soon became the focal point of the struggle.

In addition to the usual newspaper letters and articles, both parties made extensive use of mass county conventions. One of the earliest antislavery conventions was held in Maysville, Mason County, on February 12. The well-attended meeting adopted resolutions that called for "a gradual and prospective system of emancipation accompanied by colonization," and those attending pledged themselves to support only emancipation candidates. A Louisville convention had met on February 1 and adopted emancipation in principle; then it adjourned until February 12 while appropriate resolutions were drafted. The adjourned meeting adopted antislavery resolutions and called for a state emancipation convention to be held in Frankfort on April 25. In a major address William L. Breckinridge urged the people to push for colonization and not to be sidetracked from antislavery by other issues.[33]

This moderate tone was reflected in most of the other antislavery meetings. The Bowling Green assemblage on May 12

56

disavowed any interference with existing slaves but called for an absolute prohibition on importing slaves and for the deportation from the state of any slave freed in the future. This group also asked for a constitutional provision that would allow a direct popular vote upon emancipation whenever the people wanted it. Twenty-four of the forty signers of the resolutions were slaveholders, including Joseph R. Underwood.[34]

Henry Clay's failure to support the 1838 movement for a constitutional convention had helped doom it, but this time his support was available. Writing from New Orleans on February 17, 1849, Clay endorsed a cautious emancipation plan that would free at age twenty-five all slaves born after some date such as 1855 or 1860, while leaving as slaves those born earlier. The freed slaves would then be hired out by the state to earn their passage and support for their first six months in Liberia. Children born to the freed slaves would be free but could be held as apprentices until age twenty-one. Clay argued that Kentucky would be more prosperous without slavery than with it.[35] Reprinted widely, Clay's letter elicited mixed reactions, including a Trimble County demand that he resign from the United States Senate.

The Frankfort antislavery convention met on April 25 with over 150 delegates present from twenty-four counties. Cassius Clay, Robert J. Breckinridge, John G. Fee, and Joseph R. Underwood were among its more prominent members. The *Presbyterian Herald* of May 5 calculated that over half the delegates were slaveholders who owned more than 3,000 slaves. Of the twenty-one ministers present, thirteen were Presbyterians. Henry Clay of Bourbon County (not Henry Clay of Ashland) presided, but the members could not produce agreement on a plan of emancipation, although the majority favored some gradual plan, followed by colonization. The members did agree to seek the election of convention delegates who would oppose further importation of slaves and would favor the right of the people to adopt emancipation easily when they wished to do so.[36]

The campaign for convention delegates was hotly contested, and debates attracted large and attentive crowds. Cassius Clay and Robert J. Breckinridge were the stars for the emancipationists; they were opposed by such luminaries as James Guthrie, Garrett Davis, Archibald Dixon, and John C. Breckinridge, Robert J. Breckinridge's nephew. Emotions sometimes ran high, and in a postdebate argument at Paducah, Judge James Campbell killed Benedict Austin, his rival for a convention seat. Cassius Clay participated in one of the bloodiest encounters at Foxtown in Madison County on June 22. Present to support an emancipation candidate, Clay became involved in a melee with several of Squire Turner's sons. So critically wounded that he was expected to die, Clay killed Cyrus Turner with his famed bowie knife.[37]

Even a cholera epidemic that devastated the state in 1849 failed to halt the campaigning. The proslavery people had control of most of the regular party machinery. They selected moderate candidates with public appeal, drawing strength from both the Whig and Democratic parties. They controlled most of the state's newspapers, and they laughed at opponents who could not agree among themselves on what they wanted. If Kentucky should be disloyal to the South, they asserted, the result could be dissolution of the Union. The attempted escapes of thirteen slaves from Mason County and forty-two from Fayette and Bourbon counties in early August could not have aided the proslavery party more had they been staged for the purpose.

The antislavery candidates stressed economic self-interest and humanitarianism. Slaves depressed the economy and held down the wages paid white workers. As humans, slaves were entitled to such basic rights as freedom. Given an opportunity, the slave was capable of self-improvement. But, many emancipationists insisted, he could best make progress in Africa. The linkage of emancipation and colonization was an oft-stated theme.

Such arguments did not prevail. Although the Emancipation party ran candidates in 29 counties and polled 10,000 votes, it did not elect a delegate to the convention. Antislavery advocates were bitterly disappointed by the results, although such a free discussion of the issue had not been possible in Kentucky since the early 1830s.

Slavery did receive extensive examination in the convention over which James Guthrie presided. A quarter of the debates dealt with slavery, and there were critics as well as supporters of the institution. Squire Turner of Madison County touched off the slavery debate with several proslavery resolutions. Extended discussion of slave importation and the deportation of freed blacks followed, but on October 10 a committee recommended that the convention retain the slavery article from the previous constitution. Turner wanted to insert the Non-Importation Act of 1833 in the constitution, despite the fact that many antislavery advocates also favored it, but other proslavery delegates defeated reintroduction of the act they had worked for years to repeal.

Silas Woodson, later a governor of Missouri, gave the only speech that was emancipationist in tone. He opposed adding to the bill of rights the declaration that "the right of property is before and higher than any constitutional sanction, and the right of the owner of a slave to his property is the same and as inviolate as the right of the owner of any property whatsoever." The majority had the right to rule, he insisted, and the overwhelming majority of Kentuckians were non-slaveholders. The state might be ready for emancipation in the future, and then the people should be free to act. The provision he opposed "had tied slavery around the necks of Kentucky's future generations like an anchor." Ben Hardin retorted, "We promised to fix the constitution so that a majority could not oppress a minority, and we have done so." The result, as a historian has recently pointed out, was that "Kentucky's organic law was subverted by linking liberty to property, instead of the universal principles of democracy."[38]

Most of the delegates who spoke on the subject admitted that slavery was an evil, but they denied that Kentucky was ready for emancipation. The new constitution contained most of the slavery provisions of the old one, but it added the declaration that placed property rights above constitutional sanctions. No slave could be freed in the future without leaving the state, and free Negroes were forbidden to enter Kentucky.

The persistent antislavery agitators kept the issue of freedom alive in Kentucky, and it is probably true that "the free discussion of slavery both in the press and in public discussion prevailed to a greater extent than in any other slave state. . . ."[39] Yet the fact remained that the emancipationists lost badly in 1849, and the legal existence of slavery was more firmly fixed after the 1849 convention than it had been before the struggle for the convention.

4

THE DETERMINED OPPONENTS

THE DECISIVE DEFEAT suffered in 1849 discouraged many of the foes of slavery, and some of them accepted the reverse as final. Others, who could not accept life in a permanent slave community, left the state. Samuel Freeman Miller, later a member of the Supreme Court, had been an emancipationist candidate from Knox County in 1849 but had withdrawn to avoid splitting the antislavery vote. Sorely disappointed with the new constitution, he moved to Iowa where he freed all his slaves.[1] But some determined opponents of slavery refused to concede defeat and continued the struggle during the final decade before the advent of the great sectional crisis and the outbreak of the Civil War. Their failure to form a unified group was one of their major weaknesses. Some were abolitionists, some emancipationists; some believed in colonization, some did not; some were careful to work for change within the existing legal system, some ignored laws they considered immoral and unconstitutional. It was a credit to their courage and, in some degree, to Kentucky's tolerance that these opponents of slavery were able to continue their agitation during most of the troubled decade.

Calvin Fairbank was one of the abolitionists who fought slavery by trying to rescue slaves from it. Oberlin College helped make him antislavery, and he became convinced that "a higher law" called him into active opposition. Although he spent over seventeen years in prison, Fairbank proudly boasted of helping forty-seven slaves escape from Kentucky and Virginia. "I piloted them through the forests, mostly by night," he wrote, "girls, fair and white, dressed as ladies; men and boys as gentlemen, or servants—men in women's clothes, and women in men's clothes; boys dressed as girls, and girls as boys; on foot or on horseback, in buggies, carriages, common wagons, in and under loads of hay, straw, old furniture, boxes and bags; crossed the Jordan of the slave, swimming, or wading chin deep, or in boats, or skiffs, on rafts, and often on a pine log. And I never suffered one to be recaptured."[2]

Fairbank began his personal crusade in 1837 when he helped a slave escape from Virginia, but most of his efforts were devoted to Kentucky. His most noted attempt occurred in 1844 when he was in Lexington as a visiting minister. He boarded with David Glass on West Second Street; another boarder was Miss Delia A. Webster, a native of Vermont who was principal of the elite Lexington Female Academy. Discovering that they shared a hatred of slavery, they concocted a plan to free three slaves. On Saturday afternoon, September 28, Fairbank hired a hack and driver and early that evening picked up Miss Webster at their boardinghouse, ostensibly for an elopement. Instead, under cover of night they made off with Lewis and Harriet Hayden and their ten-year-old son.[3]

By driving through the night the party reached Washington in Mason County early the next morning. They remained there during the day, and after dark drove to Maysville, where they crossed the Ohio. At Ripley, Ohio, the fugitives were turned over to the Reverend John Rankin, a well-known abolitionist who had assisted many slaves in their escapes. The two whites and their black driver then started for Lexington, apparently hoping to arrive before the escape was discovered.

But a search had already begun, and they were seized when they reached Paris. Rushed to Lexington, they were put in Thomas B. Megowan's slave jail. Fairbank was placed in irons after an unsuccessful escape attempt. After a severe whipping,

Isaac, the elderly slave driver of the hack, confessed that he had carried the fugitives. A search of the boardinghouse provided written evidence of their involvement, and the abolitionists were indicted in Fayette Circuit Court for "aiding and enticing slaves to leave their owners & to escape beyond the limits of this town, viz to Ohio." The community's sense of outrage increased when Lewis wrote his master from Canada, "I have concluded for the present to try Freedom & how it will seem to be my own Master & Manage my own matters & crack my own whip. . . . I am willing to labour, but am desirous to act the Gentleman."

When the trial opened on December 17, Miss Webster was represented by three prominent attorneys while Fairbank had only a court-appointed lawyer. In an ungenerous gesture, Miss Webster objected to being tried with Fairbank, "fearing the prejudice that existed against *him* would impair my case." She denied guilt and insisted she was the innocent victim of his activities. He was tried separately after her protest. The minister changed his plea to guilty but sought the mercy of the court on the grounds that he had been reared as an abolitionist who believed slavery was wrong. After five days of intense courtroom excitement, the jury found both defendants guilty. Miss Webster was sentenced to two years in the state penitentiary; the Reverend Fairbank received fifteen years, five for each slave.

The incarceration of a gentlewoman, even though she was an abolitionist, aroused considerable public sympathy upon which Miss Webster played to the fullest possible extent. Governor William Owsley, warned in late December by the clerk of the Fayette Circuit Court that "the state of public opinion here is strong & decisive against any extension of Executive clemency *at this time*," denied her initial requests for either a pardon or a new trial, but she received exceptionally lenient treatment. A small house was erected for her comfort; she could spend her time as she wished and receive visitors at will. The governor called several times, and jailor Newton Craig was so friendly that he was suspected of a romantic attachment. Owsley waited for public excitement to subside and then pardoned Miss Webster after she had served just six weeks of her sentence.

Fairbank endured a quite different experience. Dressed in prison stripes, his head shaven, he worked at sawing stone and cobbling shoes; after his health failed, he became a hospital steward. When Governor John J. Crittenden granted a pardon on August 23, 1849, Fairbank had served nearly five years.

Kentucky had not seen the last of this abolitionist duo. In November 1851, Calvin Fairbank was arrested in Jeffersonville, Indiana, on charges of having abducted Tamar, a young mulatto girl whose Louisville master planned to sell her. Fairbank complained that he was kidnapped in Indiana by three Kentuckians who carried him across the Ohio to face trial. He was not surprised to be found guilty again, but he claimed that the jury added up the sentences suggested by each member, divided the total by twelve, and gave him another fifteen years. According to his statistics he was whipped 1,003 times for a total of 35,105 lashes before he was pardoned in 1864, having served just over twelve years. His normal 180 pounds had declined to 117½, and when he reached Cincinnati some of his former associates did not recognize him.

Miss Webster returned to Kentucky during the winter of 1853–1854, when she used abolitionist funds to purchase a 600-acre farm in Trimble County on the Ohio River. Its ostensible purpose was to demonstrate the superiority of free labor, but so many slaves disappeared from the neighborhood that fifty slaveholders soon demanded that she leave the state. She was put in the Bedford County jail in the spring when she refused to post $10,000 bond to guarantee her departure. Released a few weeks later on a writ of habeas corpus, she was indicted in June in Trimble County for helping slaves escape. Learning of her impending arrest, Miss Webster fled to Indiana. The farm was sold for debt, and the "petticoat abolitionist" did not return to Kentucky again.

A different campaign against slavery was waged by William Shreve Bailey, a mechanic-turned-editor, who continued the journalistic assault that Cassius Clay had used in 1845.[4] Bailey had opened a machine shop in Newport in 1839. A man of independent thought, he became converted to immediate abolition and began writing articles for the *Newport News* to advance his opinions. The articles caused so much adverse comment that the harassed editor of the *Newport News* suggested that Bailey purchase his printing plant. A deal was made for $650, and in March 1850 the mechanic-editor began publication of an antislavery paper that changed names several times but was best known as the *Newport News* and the *Free South*. Bailey's chief argument was economic, and he made a particular appeal to working-class whites. Some needed support came from northern abolitionists, but John G. Fee, sent by the American Missionary Association to appraise the paper, gave an adverse report because Bailey did not subscribe to Fee's antislavery principles. The editor was usually in financial straits, but ten of his children could set type, and he managed to continue operations.

Editing an abolitionist newspaper in a slaveholding state was bad enough, but Bailey compounded his crime by supporting the Republican party after its formation in 1854. He devoted considerable space to such national events as the Kansas-Nebraska Act, the struggle over Kansas, and the Dred Scott decision, and on all of them he followed the principles of the new party. Boycotts by proslavery advertisers resulted in critical losses of revenue, and his building was burned in October 1851 by a mob. Lawsuits were filed against him, and Bailey had to pay $300 damages in a libel case. When he beat up an assailant who tried to cane him, Bailey was sued by his victim. The real crisis came after John Brown's raid on Harper's Ferry which the *Covington Journal* of October 22, 1859, called an example of "practical Abolitionism." On the evening of October 28 another mob moved Bailey's presses into the street and threw most of the type into the gutter. Some articles were stolen the next night, and Bailey was warned to leave the state at once. Unawed by the threats, he sought northern support to reestablish his press, and he sued those responsible for the damages. As for leaving, he replied that he would "only go *dead*, and that *some* of them at least must die with me in the struggle."

"Arms are more respected here than *law*," he declared bitterly, "and I find that those who use them are more esteemed than non-resistants." When he resumed publication Bailey was arrested for incendiary writings. Northern supporters provided bail and then sent him to England to solicit antislavery funds. When he returned home the Civil War had started and the charges were dropped. Bailey lacked the wealth and prestige of some other antislavery Kentuckians, but his persistent opposition was one of the most courageous examples of antislavery agitation that Kentucky witnessed.

In late 1855 a New England teacher named J. Brady announced that he would start an antislavery newspaper in Lexington. The citizens were determined not to allow another *True American* to develop, and a mob consisting largely of poor whites who indicated a desire "to taste the blood of an Abolitionist" chased Brady out of town as city officials refused to protect him. A few years later the General Assembly tried to provide legal sanction for suppressing antislavery publications by voting a prison sentence for "any free person [to] write or print, or cause to be written or printed, any book or other thing, with intent to advise or incite negroes in this State to rebel or make insurrections," and knowingly to circulate the same.[5]

Once recovered from the wounds received in the Turner fight, Cassius Clay resumed his struggle with slavery and its adherents, but this time he concentrated upon politics; he made no effort to resurrect the *True American*. Clay had left the Whigs after the 1848 campaign, and in the early 1850s he helped destroy that once-proud party. Clay had become well known nationally and he had political ambitions; thus, much of his time was devoted to northern speaking tours. He had come to believe that only a national solution would end slavery, and he obviously enjoyed the flattering attention he received north of the Mason-Dixon line. As the nation lurched from crisis to crisis, Clay deluded himself into believing that he might attain

66

high office, perhaps even the presidency of the United States.

In 1851, however, Clay focused attention on the state gubernatorial race. He announced the formation of the Emancipation party and called for a convention to nominate candidates. When the convention failed to meet, he declared himself the candidate and invited Dr. George D. Blakey of Logan County to run for lieutenant governor. Clay did not expect to win, but he hoped to get as many as ten thousand votes that would provide a political base for the future. And since most of his votes would come from the Whigs, he hoped to ensure their defeat. He and Blakey conducted an active campaign with at least one of them speaking in each county. They stressed legal, gradual emancipation, and they sought the support of non-slaveholders. Clay was disappointed when he received only 3,621 votes (Blakey had 1,670), but he was convinced that his candidacy allowed Democrat Lazarus W. Powell to defeat Whig Archibald Dixon by a margin of 850 votes.[6]

Cassius Clay did not run again for public office, but he worked to keep alive a small antislavery party that became the nucleus of Kentucky's Republican party after 1854, when this new sectional party was formed. He apparently met Abraham Lincoln for the first time in 1854 when Clay spoke at Springfield, Illinois. With characteristic modesty, Clay later claimed credit for Lincoln's antislavery views: "I flatter myself that I sowed good seed in good ground, which, in the providence of God, produced in good time good fruit." In April 1856 the Madison County Republicans held a convention to select delegates for the national convention and to form a local organization. Clay's draft statement, which the group adopted, called slavery a state matter but urged Kentuckians to use all moral and political means to end it.[7] Kentucky was a lost cause for the Republicans, but Clay was extremely active elsewhere during the campaign, particularly in the states of the Old Northwest.

He came out of the campaign with an enhanced national reputation and with expanded hopes for future preference within the party. In the 1860 Republican convention Cassius Clay received two votes for president on the second ballot and, after Lincoln's nomination, was a strong second to Hannibal Hamlin of Maine for the vice-presidential nomination. But his geographical location and antislavery reputation made him a poor choice, despite popular support from the spectators. During the campaign Clay spoke tirelessly on behalf of the party, mostly in the northern states. Convinced that he had had a major role in securing the Republican victory, Clay anticipated receiving one of the more prestigious cabinet posts. In the end he had to console himself with an appointment as minister to Russia.

While Clay was increasingly active in national politics, he did not abandon the state scene. After 1851 he began to seek supporters from the hills and mountains east and south of the Bluegrass, where the people owned few slaves and possessed a traditional animosity toward the lowlanders. Since most of them owned their farms, they were largely immune from the economic pressure that could be exerted upon hired workmen in other areas of the state. As Clay turned his attention toward that region, he became an uneasy ally of John G. Fee and a group of associates who were also committed to the overthrow of slavery. For a few years Clay and Fee formed an unusual partnership in their struggle to rid the state of slavery.

John G. Fee was born in Bracken County on September 9, 1816, into a slaveholding, staunchly Presbyterian family. He was educated at Augusta College and Miami University before entering Lane Seminary in 1842. At Lane he underwent the spiritual conversion to abolitionism that determined the course of his antislavery career. "Lord, if needs be, make me an Abolitionist," Fee prayed in a grove near the seminary. When the call came he decided to return to Kentucky and fight the evil there. His decision to return may have been hastened by another call. Appalled by his son's attitude, Fee's father wrote: "Dear son: Bundle up your books and come home; I have spent the last dollar I mean to spend on you in a free state." [8] Fee represented the evangelical aspect of the antislavery movement, a side that was missing in the appeals of such antislavery advocates as Cassius Clay. Fee believed that a religious conversion should also add a recruit to the crusade against slavery. As he wrote Lewis Tappan on June 10, 1847, "In whatever way we enter our protest against slavery it must be for the good reason that it is sin against God."

Fee's first failure came when he failed to convert his father, who armed himself with proslavery books and pamphlets to refute his son's arguments. The young minister spurned calls from several Bracken County churches that wanted him to ignore the slavery issue. His first church, at Cabin Creek in Lewis County, had just five members, two of whom withdrew when their pastor's outspoken criticism of slavery aroused opposition. He antagonized the advocates of colonization when he declared that "to banish a man from the land of his birth, guilty of no crime, was gross injustice." In his first church Fee established a principle from which he would not deviate. "In our church we have no slave holders," he once wrote, "nor as long as I am pastor of it, will there be any."[9] As a consequence of this adamant stand, the New School Presbyterian Synod dismissed him in 1845. He and his few followers styled themselves a nondenominational "Church of Christ," but when Fee decided that he should be rebaptized he called upon a North Carolina Baptist to perform the immersion.

Preaching before small groups, asked to move by his landlord, deprived of the $200 that had come each year from the American Home Missionary Society, estranged from his family, Fee received some support from Cassius Clay to whom he wrote in 1844 to introduce himself.[10] Although they differed on how to end slavery, their relations were cordial in the mid-1840s, and Fee wrote several articles for the *True American*. The minister's financial plight was relieved in 1848 when he was employed by the American Missionary Association. Organized at Albany, New York, in 1846 the association enlisted the active participation of such noted abolitionists as George Whipple, Simon S. Jocelyn, and the Tappan brothers, Lewis and Arthur. While its constitution did not stress antislavery, the association soon concentrated on that cause. Membership was limited to evangelical churches and their members, and agents were recruited largely through Oberlin College connections. While some work was done among Indians and abroad, most of their efforts centered upon anti-slavery agitation in the midwestern states. The association stressed noncommunion with slaveholders and nonviolence in its efforts to abolish slavery.[11] The association and Fee were well met; he provided leadership for the work in Kentucky, and the association gave him support without which he might have been forced to leave the state at an early date.

By the early 1850s Fee's reports were increasingly optimistic. The tiny Cabin Creek congregation had grown to 35 members, and 100 people often attended the services. Blessed by unaccustomed affluence, the church had been able to pay Fee as much as sixty-one dollars for the year. A new church that drew as many as 150 persons to services had been founded in Bracken County, and despite threats Fee preached there and in a number of other communities. True to his tenets, Fee wrote, "I carry no weapons; I know retaliation will destroy society. If I suffer I will make my appeal to the civil courts." He began building new churches to house his two growing congregations, and he was delighted when both groups voted to admit blacks on an equal basis with whites. The work expanded so rapidly that Fee requested the American Missionary Association to send another missionary into the area. "I am now more than ever convinced that an anti-slavery gospel can be preached and will succeed in Kentucky," he told his headquarters.[12]

During the 1850s Fee drew upon his previous articles and sermons to publish three pamphlets that gave a summary of his antislavery views. *An Anti-Slavery Manual; Or, The Wrongs of American Slavery Exposed by the Light of the Bible and of Facts, with a Remedy for the Evil* (1851) was the most comprehensive. Fee exercised his biblical scholarship to refute assertions that the Bible sanctioned slavery, and he argued in Enlightenment terms that "freedom is the natural state of all men, as soon as they attain the age of manhood." This belief allowed him to appeal to "a higher law" when forced to admit that slavery was legal in the United States. Fee attacked slavery on economic grounds also, but this phase of his argument was subordinate to his moral objections. He flatly rejected the efforts of the Colonization Society: "Colonization will never remove slavery." The two later publications added little to the arguments of the first one, although in the third Fee presented a defense of the policy of nonfellowship with slaveholders.

In 1854 Fee transferred his efforts to Madison County. Cassius Clay, who was trying to build a political base in that area, was at least partially responsible for the move. Fee visited Clay in 1853 and preached several times in the neighborhood. He was shocked by what he saw of the work of Wiley Fisk, another American Missionary Association missionary. Fisk's responsibilities were too great for one man to handle, but he condemned himself in Fee's eyes by carrying a revolver, trading horses, and chewing tobacco. (He was later accused, probably unjustly, of adultery.) Many church members insisted that Fee become their pastor. Clay urged him to make the change, and in 1854 Fee moved to Madison County. Clay gave him ten acres of poor land on which to build a house, and church members donated their labor in lieu of his first year's salary. Fee called his new home "Berea" after the Berea of Macedonia where the people received the words of Paul "with all readiness of mind."

The local people employed as colporters to distribute tracts and Bibles did not work out well, and Fee persuaded the association to send in both colporters and missionaries from the North. There were some unfortunate selections, but such men as George Candee, Otis B. Waters, and John A. R. Rogers were invaluable helpers in Fee's exciting new endeavors. The Bereans were deeply concerned with education, partly because they believed that learning would result in the rejection of slavery, partly because they believed that everyone should be able to read the Bible. Since the region had few schools, they started building some at once. Their schools were usually associated with a church, and antislavery ideals pervaded both. Black students were sometimes enrolled along with whites, and the school that Otis Waters taught at Berea included young men as well as children, for many of the area's adults were illiterate. As soon as possible the young men were

71

sent out to teach and to expound the antislavery gospel in other isolated communities.

Fee was not satisfied with the educational progress that was being made; more facilities were needed, offering work at a higher level than the elementary classes. "We need a college here," he told the American Missionary Association in January 1857, "one which shall be to Kentucky what Oberlin . . . is to Ohio; an anti-slavery, anti-caste, anti-rum, anti-tobacco, anti-sectarian, pious school under Christian influence, a school that will furnish the best possible facilities for those with small means, who have energy of character that will lead them to work their way through this world. We need working men. The rich, the proud and the indolent will not come to such a school as we propose." Berea College was founded on these principles.

Fee was essentially a minister, not a teacher, but he was fortunate in having John A. R. Rogers available to help start the school. Before even meeting Fee, Rogers had come to Kentucky with a dream of establishing a college. A remarkable mathematician and a fine linguist, Rogers was the true academic leader of the institution that was called Berea. He was also skilled in dealing with opponents of the community and school. One of his most effective techniques was to take his wife to visit an outspoken critic just before mealtime. Kentucky hospitality would demand that they be fed, and Rogers often broke down an opponent's initial resistance at the table.[13]

Fee, Rogers, John Hanson (Fee's cousin), and a few others met at Fee's home on September 7, 1858, to plan the proposed college. Rogers chaired the committee that drafted a constitution based on Fee's principles. The admission of blacks caused some discussion, but Rogers and Fee were adamant on the point, and when an election was held for district trustees supporters of the radical proposal won by a nearly three-to-one margin. (But no blacks applied when the college first opened.) In 1859 the school purchased 110 acres for $1,750 in an area of such thick brush that it was said "a rabbit could not get through without pinning back his ears."[14]

The Bereans asked the American Missionary Association for $300 to help meet the expense, and Fee attended the association's annual meeting in a search for possible donors. Progress was being made, but soon Berea faced a major crisis.

Fee had encountered opposition for his antislavery views wherever he preached, and Madison County was no exception. In the spring of 1855 he was scheduled for a debate near Crab Orchard on the topic of colonization, but a heavily armed mob intervened. Its members hooted at his claim to free speech and ignored his demands that their differences be settled in a court of law. When Fee refused to leave the house in which he was preaching, he was dragged outside, put on his horse, and driven off. The grand jury refused to indict because it might "produce excitement." Cassius Clay, charging that the act had really been aimed at him, offered to escort Fee with a hundred armed men to Rockcastle County for another speech. Fee rejected the offer, but he and Clay spoke there on the appointed day despite ominous warnings to remain away.

It would have been difficult to find two such diverse characters in pursuit of a common goal. Clay was notorious for his bloody personal encounters but moderate in his antislavery views; he obeyed laws until they could be changed, and he compromised when he could not secure all he sought. Fee prayed for members of mobs who manhandled him, but he ignored laws that he considered unjust. "Iniquitous laws should be broken," he declared. He felt his principles compromised when Clay strode into one of his difficult meetings and roared, "This preacher is going to have a fair hearing!" Fee reproved Clay frequently for swearing and drinking; they spent much of their time together in personal disputes. Their basic difference was over the best way to end slavery. Fee was an abolitionist, Clay an emancipationist, and there was a vast difference between their views. Clay gradually became convinced that Fee's radicalism was preventing moderates from joining Clay's party.

The ill-assorted pair disagreed openly at a July 4 celebration at Slate Lick Spring in 1856, when Fee condemned the harsh Fugitive Slave Act of 1850 that had been a major concession to the South. "A law confessedly contrary to the law of God ought not by human courts be enforced," he declared as he vowed not to obey it. Then Clay warned the audience that Fee's views were illegal and dangerous. Good citizens were bound to obey a law of which they disapproved until it was repealed. By the time they ended their discussion, Fee wrote, "There was manifest confusion in the crowd." A partial reconciliation was effected in 1858, but Fee and Clay were never as close as they had been before the July 4 dispute. The withdrawal of Clay's support left the Bereans more vulnerable to the proslavery element.

In June 1857 a new church was founded in Rockcastle County, and on July 20 another mob dragged Fee from the house in which he was preaching. He was escorted out of the county, but the mob's enthusiasm had waned by the time they reached Crab Orchard, and Fee was released to return to his anxious family and friends. There was little harassment thereafter until January 16, 1858, when a rowdy group of thirty to fifty men interrupted Fee's service at Lewis Chapel in Madison County. He and Robert Jones, a colporter for the American Missionary Association, were seized and threatened with drowning unless they agreed to leave the county. Jones was severely whipped, but then the abashed mob turned them loose. Fee tried again to secure indictments against the mob's leaders, but local authorities would not act. One of his daughters later recalled, "We children never thought anything more about mobs than about thunderstorms. We supposed everybody had mobs!"[15] Fee did derive a great deal of un-Christian satisfaction in keeping track of the gruesome accidents that befell those who had interfered with his work.

During another lull in the harassment, Berea College opened in the fall of 1858, and new converts and buildings alike testified to the growth of the community. But the peace was broken after October 1859, when John Brown's raid on Harper's Ferry spread fear and consternation throughout the slave states. Fee was on a fund-raising tour of the East at the time, and soon after the event he referred to it while preaching in Henry Ward Beecher's Brooklyn church. "We want more John Browns," Fee said, "not in manner of action but in spirit of consecration; not to go with carnal weapons, but with spiritual; men who, with Bibles in their hands, and tears in their eyes, will beseech man to be reconciled to God. Give us such men, and we may yet save the South."[16]

The *Louisville Daily Courier* of November 17, either intentionally or as a result of poor reporting, quoted Fee as saying that "more John Browns were wanted, especially for Kentucky." Other papers added to the distortion, and wild rumors swept across the state. A stream of northern immigrants was reported flowing into Berea with massive trunks that contained weapons with which to arm slaves for a major revolt. The excitement did not subside when "an infernal machine" consigned to Berea turned out to be a set of candle molds. Learning of the absurd charges, Fee sent a circular "To the Citizens of Madison County, Kentucky" in which he attempted to correct the statement for which he was blamed and to explain just what he had meant. He and his friends opposed slavery, and they were willing to defend their position in any court of law. "If slavery be right," Fee challenged, "it will abide the test, if not, it is for the highest interests of all, that it should pass away, by means that are at once legitimate and righteous."[17]

His explanations were ignored by the proslavery forces who saw an opportunity to dislodge the Bereans from their foothold. On December 23, 1859, a committee of sixty men visited Rogers and the other Bereans. Ignoring explanations and protests, the committee ordered them to leave Kentucky within ten days. The threatened group sought solace in a prayer meeting at which Hanson read from Psalm 37: "Fret not thyself because of evil-doers, neither be thou envious against the workers of iniquity. For they shall soon be cut down like the grass, and wither as the green herb. Trust in the Lord, and do good; so shall thou decide in the land, and verily thou shall be fed."

The Bereans also appealed to Beriah Magoffin for protection, but the proslavery governor replied that he could give no aid. Fee's "Circular No. 2" had no more effect than the first one, and even their friends suggested a temporary withdrawal for the Berea settlers. Years later Elizabeth Rogers described that period for her children. "It required great courage in those early days to send your father off on his Sunday trips. . . . There were rumors of attack and mob violence and I sent him off more than once wondering if my goodbye kiss was for the trip, or for the last time." Conditions had become worse after John Brown's raid. "I had lain awake nights trembling at every noise, and I had stood terror stricken before the drunken crowd who used to swagger up and down our streets, but there was a more savage element than ever before in the threats toward us."[18]

In the absence of Fee, Rogers was the key figure in the decision to leave. "If we had determined to remain," he explained, "a civil war very possibly might have been the result," for their supporters "would have rallied to the side of free speech." But violence was against their principles, and by the end of December a motley caravan of three dozen people was on its way to Cincinnati, where Fee joined them. But, as Rogers said, "We all expected to return and complete the work we had begun, but how & when we knew not, & could not know."[19] The Berea experiment had ended until after the Civil War, except for the impact that it had already had upon the minds and souls of the mountaineers it had touched.

The expulsion was approved across the state by public meetings and editorials. The citizens who attended a meeting at Orangeburg in Mason County on January 21, 1860, resolved that "no Abolitionist has a right to establish himself in the slaveholding community and disseminate opinions and principles destructive of its tranquillity and safety." Kentuckians had not interfered with northern rights, and "we desire and demand to be 'let alone,' leaving our officious and philanthropic friends at the North and elsewhere to work out their personal and social salvation with fear and trembling."[20]

The expulsion presented Cassius Clay with a dilemma. He wanted to disassociate himself from any connection with the exiles, but he had the reputation of defending free speech and he had supported the group in the past. Clay touched upon the problem in a major address delivered in Frankfort on January 10, 1860. Refused use of the house chamber, he made a dramatic three-hour appearance on the steps of the Capitol in a rain that soaked but did not dispel a large audience. He could not accept Fee's concept of "the higher law," Clay said, but he defended Fee against the charges that he had planned a slave insurrection. He paid tribute to Fee's work, although his description of the pre-Berea inhabitants as "a drunken, tobacco-chewing and whiskey-drinking people" was a bit unkind. Fee and his associates had changed that, Clay said. "The children, before idle and dissipated, had long since reformed, and were going to the best schools in the country. . . ." As a result of Fee's efforts, "there were not better people in the State than were those surrounding the colony of Berea."[21] Despite his lavish praise, the fact remained that the Bereans were in exile and Clay had made no effort to protect them.

John Hanson returned to Berea in the spring of 1860 to look after his sawmill, but when he attracted attention by attending Sunday school and preaching, a mob came after him. Hanson escaped, but his sawmill and a house in which he was suspected of hiding were burned. When some local citizens armed themselves for protection, the mob asked for cannon from Lexington. With his usual capacity for self-delusion Clay decided that he was the true target of the mob, and in speech and print he again disassociated himself from the higher-law abolitionists.[22] Hanson escaped to Ohio, and he and the other Bereans scattered to spread the news of their mission and ordeal throughout the North until the day when they could return.

When the 1860 presidential election was held, Kentucky's slaves still seemed a long way from freedom. Lincoln and the Republican party were absolutely opposed to the expansion of slavery, but they pledged noninterference within the states that already had it. Republican Cassius Clay had become a national figure, but in 1860 Abraham Lincoln polled just 1,364 votes in the state of his birth. The experiment at Berea had ended in exile, although George Candee remained in Jackson County until April 1861, when he was forced to leave. Then the only association missionary left in Kentucky was the largely ineffective William Mobley. The constitution of 1849 was still in effect with no foreseeable chance of amending its proslavery sections. It may be that in the late 1850s Kentucky's antislavery advocates had more freedom of expression than those in any other slave state. If true, the statement is more a reflection of the deplorable situation in other states than it is praise for the Kentucky attitude. In 1860 slavery appeared as firmly fastened upon the state as it had been at any time since statehood was achieved.

5

BLACKS AGAINST SLAVERY

Much of the writing about the antislavery movement has concentrated upon the whites who participated in it. When blacks are mentioned, they are usually treated merely as subjects of the movement, not as active participants in it. But the blacks were the people most directly and most intimately associated with slavery. They were the ones who suffered most from it, and they stood to gain most from its extinction. Many of Kentucky's slaves opposed the institution in some way, and most of them displayed their opposition without assistance from antislavery whites.

When the black role in the antislavery movement has not been ignored, it has often been interpreted to fit preconceived ideas. Some proponents of the system depicted slavery as such a benevolent institution that the people fortunate enough to be slaves were too happy and contented with their status to want to leave it. Some opponents of slavery endowed each slave with such burning desire for freedom that the South was in constant turmoil as slaves sought to overturn or escape from their bondage. Neither extreme view is correct.

In his study of the underground railroad Larry Gara pointed out that most slaves adjusted to slavery instead of trying to escape from it. "Given the conditions of their time," he said, "most of the bondsmen had little alternative to some kind of adjustment within the slave society. Very few of them allowed any hope of freedom they may have harbored to lead to deeds. The chances of a successful escape from the South were indeed remote, and few would risk the ordeal of a flight to the North."[1] Eugene D. Genovese has argued convincingly that the "Sambo" personality was a feature of slavery wherever it existed, although "a seemingly docile slave could suddenly turn fierce." Since each system of slavery contained countering influences, some favoring and others thwarting overt opposition, the important question was: Under what conditions was the docile slave likely to be transformed?[2]

The most common form of resistance to Kentucky slavery was the practice of doing as little as possible to benefit the master. The ideal was to do just enough well enough to avoid punishment. Shrewd masters sometimes tried to overcome this slowdown by encouraging contests between individuals and work gangs or by providing incentives of money, goods, or free time when an assigned quota had been satisfactorily completed. As a result of such measures, some slaves were able to purchase their freedom. In 1835 Cincinnati was reported to have 1,129 free blacks; of this number, 476 were said to have bought their freedom. A number of these freemen had been slaves in Kentucky.[3]

Feigning illness was another oft-used technique for avoiding work. Masters were understandably suspicious of sudden illnesses that struck just before a hard piece of work began, and the initial treatment was likely to be some heroic remedy such as caster oil, the very suggestion of which sometimes produced miraculous recoveries. A few slaves resorted to self-mutilation to end their days at hard labor. Cutting tendons in the leg or ankle was probably the most common method used, but there were instances in which fingers and even hands were amputated.

The ultimate form of self-molestation was suicide, and some Kentucky slaves found in death an escape from the tribulations of slavery. Ex-slave Sophia Word told of a nearby master who was so cruel that two female slaves killed themselves. "One nigger gal Sudie wuz found across the bed with a pen knife in her hand. He whipped another nigger gal most to death, for fergiting to put onions in the stew. The next day she went down to the river and for nine days they searched for her and her body finally washed upon the shore."[4] Suicides were most common after an unsuccessful escape attempt, or when a family was being separated, or when a slave was faced with severe punishment. Yet while few reliable statistics are available, the suicide rate among slaves seems to have been lower than it was among whites in the South.[5]

Slaves also fought back against their masters and the institution of slavery by deliberate destruction of property. Tools were frequently broken or lost, horses and mules were often mistreated or broken down, and crops were stolen or destroyed. Fire was a favorite weapon, capable of great destruction but difficult to trace, and the incidence of fires was high in most slave communities although in Kentucky a slave found guilty of arson could be hanged.

Stealing, a favorite slave weapon, was so common that whites accepted a reasonable amount as a matter of course; the problem was to hold it within bounds. A distinction was often made between two types of theft: stealing goods in order to sell them was a serious matter, while taking food or other necessities for the slave's own use was generally considered acceptable. Meat disappeared from smokehouses, corn from cribs, chickens from roosts, sweets from the kitchen, despite all efforts to guard them. Some masters admitted that hunger was the main reason why food was taken, but in most cases it was not actual hunger as much as a desire for variety or just another way of getting back at Ole Massa.

Physical violence was a form of slave protest much more frightening to whites. It might range from a blow to murder, but in any form it was regarded as one of the more serious slave crimes. Farms have a wide variety of implements that can serve as weapons, and a desperate slave who was willing to bear the consequences of his action had a very good chance of wounding or killing a hated master or overseer. Assaulting a white, regardless of provocation, was punished quickly and severely. Jim Kizzie, a Henderson County overseer, was notorious for his frequent use of a rawhide whip. Driven to desperation by his floggings, several slaves attacked him on August 4, 1862, and strangled him with a noose made from their cotton suspenders. Five slaves were charged with murder, but only David, judged to be the ringleader, was hanged. As usual, a number of slaveholders marched their slaves to the execution site on February 6, 1863, to witness his death.[6] Even in such serious cases as this, the slave's economic value provided some protection, for only one of several who participated in the murder was executed.

Poison was easily available in many homes and desperate slaves sometimes used it, although the list of suspects in such cases was usually quite small. In an 1849 Fayette County case a slave named Cassilly mixed powdered glass with the gravy she served her master and mistress, and in 1858 a ten-year-old slave girl who had been whipped poisoned several persons in the household of Mrs. Patrick Pope of Louisville.[7] The most noted case was in Cassius Clay's household when he accused Emily of trying to kill his son, Cassius, Jr.

Slave revolt was a haunting fear in any slave community. Most slaveholders and many slaves were aware of the bloody uprisings in the West Indies, and enough attempts were made in the United States to keep slave owners apprehensive. A slave plot was discovered in Lexington in 1810; the following year the Kentucky legislature made insurrection, or conspiracy to start one, a felony punishable by death. The Nat Turner revolt in Virginia in 1831 shattered any idea of slave docility and hardened the southern attitude toward antislavery advocates. A group of determined slaves could wreak death and destruction on almost any farm or plantation; victims would have small consolation in knowing that such a revolt would soon be suppressed.

Rumors of slave uprisings circulated frequently, sometimes touched off by revolts in other parts of the country, at other times apparently developing spontaneously. Regardless of origin, such rumors were taken seriously and near panic often developed for no valid reason. One such incident occurred in Bardstown and its vicinity when the word spread that on a given night the rural slaves were going to kill the whites on the farms, and then massacre everyone in the town. Major Thomas Speed was skeptical of the report, but he put his own household on guard. Extra weapons were procured; axes, pitchforks, scythes, and other deadly weapons were locked up; and on the fateful evening the doors and windows were barricaded and lookouts were posted.

Toward eleven o'clock, when Speed slipped outside to reconnoiter, he was horrified to see Jim, one of his trusted slaves, sharpening a long knife at the grindstone. The major hurried back inside and warned his family. An hour later all was still quiet, and Speed made his way quietly to Jim's cabin. There Jim sat with his knife, working industriously on corn-shuck mats that he sold in town for a quarter each. Speed stomped back to the house and ordered everyone to bed. In Bardstown the next day he denounced such alarms, and "Never again did he allow himself to be disturbed by a report of an expected 'uprising.'"[8]

Some incidents were more serious than the one that annoyed Major Speed, although Kentucky never had a slave revolt comparable to the Turner insurrection. Several of the most serious affairs came when fugitives fought in an effort to escape; they should probably not even be called revolts since the slaves' hope was to escape as quietly as possible. A wave of terror swept the Bluegrass on August 5, 1848, when people learned that seventy-five slaves, many armed, were trying to reach the Ohio River. Excitement became even more intense with the news that Patrick (Edward J.) Doyle, a Centre College student, was leading the group. A reward of $5,000 was offered for the capture of the fugitives, and scores of men armed themselves and galloped off to assist in the hunt. Contact was made north of Cynthiana, but the fugitives killed one white and beat off the others. Dismayed by the unexpected resistance, the pursuers sent to nearby towns for additional help. When reinforcements arrived, Doyle and his fugitives were surrounded in a hemp field in northern Bracken County and forced to surrender after another brisk firefight. Doyle was whisked from Cynthiana, where "an immense crowd assembled around the jail with angry threats," to the greater security of the Lexington jail. Indicted on seven charges, he pleaded guilty to one and was sentenced to twenty years at hard labor. In view of the intense excitement in the community, the most surprising aspect of the slave trial was that only three leaders were found guilty and hanged.[9]

Another panic that swept across Kentucky in 1856 had little basis in fact. The state shared a general southern rumor that a massive uprising would occur on Christmas Day. Frankfort was only one of several Kentucky towns that experienced numerous alarms during the autumn, but the slaves were perhaps more terrified than the whites. "There is at this time a perfect panic among the negroes," Orlando Brown wrote his son on September 23. "They break for home as if the devil was after them whenever the ten o'clock bell rings. Wes is almost afraid to go up town even in the day time. On Monday morning a hand bill appeared signed 'Many Citizens,' publishing a 'Black List' of about a dozen free negroes who were notified to leave town by 6 o'clock of last evening, and that has operated like a bombshell among them." Brown feared that the vigilante action might get out of hand, although he thought it had probably done some good to that point.[10]

Even greater fear pervaded the southcentral portion of the state. Some minor slave unrest at an ironworks near Clarksville, Tennessee, was escalated by rumors into a plot by 600 slaves to capture Hopkinsville and then fight northward to freedom. Slaves were accused of destroying telegraph lines and killing three whites in Christian County, and a general roundup was undertaken. A few slaves were executed before it became apparent that the insurrection was imaginary. Cadiz in Trigg County experienced a similar panic that resulted in the execution of a slave and the lynching of Solomon Young, a free black preacher, before reason returned to the community.[11] Most proslavery editors across the state blamed the new Republican party and the growing influence of abolitionists for attempting to stir up the slaves.

Another wave of unrest followed John Brown's raid in October 1859. Imaginations ran riot, and incipient revolts were seen in the most innocent acts. Masters took special precautions against their bondsmen, towns imposed or enforced curfews against blacks, the county patrols were strengthened, and Yankees who chanced to be in the state were subjected to intensive interrogation. But no major outburst occurred, and the panic soon subsided. Even by the most liberal classification of incidents, Kentucky had few slave revolts. Any realistic assessment of possibilities would have concluded that an insurrection was doomed to failure, and few slaves were desperate enough to take such a hopeless course.

Revolts might have been more frequent if escape had not provided a more practicable form of resistance to slavery. Escape was the most common recourse of slaves who reached the point that they could no longer confine their opposition to resistance within the institution. The slave who ran away was the one most likely to participate in uprisings if other avenues were closed to him. It is possible that the fugitive problem so deplored by slaveholders served as a sort of safety valve for the slave South.

Fugitives fell into two general classes. The most common was the slave who ran away with no thought of permanent escape. Faced with the prospect of a spell of intensive or unpleasant work, a slave might decide that his ultimate whipping would still make a short vacation worthwhile. Impending punishment or anger over unjust treatment led other slaves to head for the woods. Others sometimes left without permission in order to see family members from whom they had been separated or to visit the home from which they had been taken. Most short-term runaways remained in the neighborhood, usually hiding in nearby woods and often being fed by other slaves. Such fugitives, while annoying to slaveholders, posed little danger to the institution of slavery.

Infinitely more serious was the case of fugitives who fled in an effort to obtain freedom. As one of the finest students of slavery has written: "These were the slaves who, short of taking the path of insurrection, most clearly repudiated the regime; who dramatically chose freedom at the highest risk; who never let the others forget that there was an alternative to their condition. . . . They may . . . have made the greatest contribution to the spirit of collective resistance that objective conditions made possible."[12] With the state's long northern boundary touching several free states, Kentucky slaveholders were very vulnerable to escape attempts. To lose a slave meant a substantial capital loss, while even recapturing a fugitive could result in considerable expense.

Accurate statistics do not exist for fugitive slaves, but there are indications that the slaveholders' problem was more emotional and symbolic than it was extensive. Modern scholars agree that the numbers reported during the slavery era were often too large. Slaveholders might exaggerate their losses in an effort to secure more stringent fugitive slave laws, while abolitionists were sometimes overanxious to prove both their own success and the intense desire of slaves for freedom. Census figures indicate that about 1,000 slaves were reported as runaways each year in the entire South; some, of course, were probably not reported. The increase in the free black population in the North and Canada did not reflect any large influx of fugitives during the pre–Civil War era. During a United States Senate debate in 1860, Kentucky's annual loss was said to be $200,000. If that figure was approximately correct, the state's loss could not have exceeded 300 slaves per year and was probably considerably smaller. Since Kentucky had 225,000 slaves in 1860, the annual loss was relatively insignificant.[13] But a master who had lost a valuable slave did not view the matter dispassionately, and after 1850 the fugitive problem became increasingly important as a symbol of relations between the North and South.

An exasperating aspect of the problem to slaveholders was that the slave most likely to escape was a man between the ages of sixteen and thirty-five, the prime years. While many men left families behind, few married women fled unless the whole family made the attempt. Proportionately, more skilled workers escaped than unskilled; the former presumably had more information about how to escape, as well as less direct supervision. And as Frederick Douglass, himself once a fugitive, pointed out, slave resistance "was more likely to result from indulgence and rising expectations than from brutalizing severity."[14] Some kindly Kentucky masters who lost valuable slaves must have been bewildered by their "ingratitude."

The slaves who attempted flight had many reasons for doing so. Resentment and grievances often built up over a period of time, but in most instances some specific incident or threat brought about the final decision to flee. Severe punishment, or the threat of it, was one of the most common causes, as was the impending sale of a slave or the breakup of a family. Some incidents were trivial in themselves, but if they were added to an accumulation of grievances, they might push a slave into making the decision to run. And in some instances slaves were encouraged or enticed into fleeing by antislavery activists.

Indeed, one of the enduring legends of the antislavery movement has been the story of the famed Underground Railroad whose fearless agents reached into every part of the South and whisked hordes of slaves to freedom along the cleverly concealed network of escape stations while baffled slaveholders cursed in futile rage. The reality was different, particularly within the slave states. The overwhelming majority of slaves never attempted to escape, and most of those who did depended largely upon their own efforts and assistance from other blacks, not upon aid from white "conductors" and "railway agents." It was illegal to help a slave escape, and many antislavery people obeyed the law. Most of Kentucky's antislavery whites never had any contact with a fugitive slave, and some would probably have felt bound to help apprehend him had they encountered one.

Such northern abolitionists as Levi Coffin and Thomas Garrett assisted a large number of fugitives, and Coffin boasted that he was "President of the Underground Railroad." Oberlin College in Ohio was antislavery from its founding, and fugitives who reached that area were almost assured of help. But the narratives of fugitive slaves indicate that most of them knew nothing of the Underground Railroad and had not been in contact with an abolitionist prior to their escapes. After Henry Bibb ran away in 1837, a Negro told him that the abolitionists would help him. "This was the first time in my life that ever I had heard of such people being in existence," Bibb said. "I supposed that they were a different race of people." When Josiah Henson led his family to freedom in 1830, he knew of people in Cincinnati who would aid them, but "they dared look to no one for help" in getting there. Fugitives were safer in seeking assistance from other slaves and free blacks than in approaching whites, but during his escape-filled career Henry Bibb was betrayed at least twice by other blacks.[15] The truth was that aid was available to most fugitives only after they had completed the most dangerous and most difficult part of their escape.

Lewis Clarke, who escaped from Kentucky slavery in 1841, was later asked how he and other slaves learned about the free states and the prospects of obtaining freedom in them. There were many ways, he answered. Personal slaves often accompanied members of the white family into free states and learned about them firsthand. Visitors from the North sometimes imparted information, and free blacks often possessed knowledge that slaves lacked. But, he added, "slaves learn most of all from hearing their masters talk." He might have added that with slave literacy higher in Kentucky than in most slave states, some information was disseminated through publications. Masters often made a point of misinforming slaves about the dangers involved in escaping and living in free areas. According to Lewis Clarke, "The master tells him, that abolitionists *decoy* slaves off into the free states, to catch them and sell them to Louisiana and Mississippi; and if he goes to Canada, the British will put *him in a mine under ground, with both eyes put out, for life.*"[16]

Lewis was born in Madison County in 1800, the son of a white father and a mulatto mother. After years of harsh treatment with different masters, he decided to escape: "I had long thought and dreamed of liberty; was now determined to make an effort, to gain it." He and a fellow slave named Isaac planned to run off in 1841 with Lewis passing as a white man and Isaac as his body servant. But Lewis feared that he could not play the role and returned home. When he left two weeks later, he rode his pony to Lexington where he visited one of his brothers. Then he started for the Ohio River, disguised by a pair of green spectacles that nearly blinded him. Once across the river he made his way to Cleveland, where he finally found a boat that carried him to Canada. Near Chatham he saw two black soldiers who had a white man in custody. "I thought then," Lewis said, "sure enough, this is the land for me."

Hearing that his brother Milton, who had escaped the previous year, was at Oberlin, Lewis went there to work. In July 1842 Lewis crossed the Ohio at Ripley and made his way by back roads to Lexington to rescue another brother, Cyrus, whose wife, a free black, elected to remain behind. Cyrus hated to walk and wanted to take two horses, but a horrified Lewis reminded him that if they were caught, horse stealing would be punished more severely than running away. Walking at night, they lost their way, grew hungry, and mired down in heavy mud. A dejected Cyrus responded unhappily to Lewis's encouragement: "Yes, freedom is good, Lewis, but this is a hard, h-a-r-d way to get it." But they persevered and reached Oberlin safely. Still apprehensive about being caught, Cyrus went on to Canada, but he did not like that area and soon returned to Ohio. Lewis went to Massachusetts in 1843 and became a popular figure on the antislavery lecture circuit where he was sometimes joined by Milton.[17]

Josiah Henson, sometimes said to be Harriet Beecher Stowe's model for Uncle Tom, also had a fascinating experience as a fugitive. Born in Maryland in 1789, he was sent to Kentucky in 1825 in charge of twenty-one other slaves his master was trying to hide from creditors. Although urged to escape at Cincinnati, Josiah fulfilled the promise made to his master and delivered the group to Amos Riley, his master's brother in Daviess County. Three years later his master ordered all his slaves in Kentucky sold except Henson and his family, and this heartless act drastically altered Josiah's views: "From that hour I saw through, hated and cursed the whole system of slavery."

In 1829 Henson, who had started preaching as a Methodist minister, returned to Maryland and purchased his freedom for $350 in cash and a note for $100. But his former master falsely declared that Henson still owed $650, and he was held in bondage despite his free status and sent back to Daviess County. When Henson decided to escape, his wife was so terrified by the prospect that he had to threaten to take their children without her before she reluctantly agreed to make the attempt. Their careful planning included practice in carrying two of their small children in knapsacks. Determined not to be retaken, Henson purchased two pistols and a knife from a poor white. A fellow slave rowed them across the Ohio, then, walking by night and hiding by day, they spent two miserable weeks getting to Cincinnati where help was secured. Their trek northward was also difficult, but on October 28, 1830, they reached Canada. "I threw myself on the ground," Henson recalled, "rolled in the sand, seized handfuls of it and kissed them, and danced round till, in the eyes of several who were present, I passed for a madman."

Henson found farm work, continued to preach, and was taught to read by a son, but his thoughts dwelt on Kentucky friends and ". . . I at once proceeded to take measures to free as many as I could." He began the dangerous game of slipping back into Kentucky, encouraging slaves to escape, and escorting them to freedom. When his memoirs were published in 1858 "Father" Henson claimed that he had assisted 118 slaves to escape "out of the cruel and merciless grasp of the slaveholder." He was active in Canada in providing better educational and economic opportunities for his fellow blacks. Henson raised money for his enterprises by frequent lecture tours in the northeastern United States and at least one extended trip to England.[18]

Some fugitives were caught and returned to slavery. Peter Bruner's inability to follow the North Star was a major handicap. "I always took the wrong direction," he wrote, explaining why he was recaptured four times without getting outside the state. "Instead of going north to the free states I went farther and farther south, just the opposite direction from which I wanted to go." Ordinarily good-natured, his master became so provoked by Peter's frequent efforts to escape that whippings became severe. This inept fugitive finally succeeded in his attempts during the Civil War when he heard that Union officers were enlisting black soldiers at Camp Nelson, only forty-one miles away. Peter managed to navigate that distance without getting lost, and on July 25, 1864, he enlisted in the artillery.[19]

Other escape attempts ended in tragedy. In late January 1856 eight members of the Garner slave family and nine friends managed to get from Boone County to an assumed haven in Cincinnati. But someone betrayed them, and pursuers broke into the house in which they were hidden. As they did so, Mary Garner, unwilling to see her children returned to slavery, killed the youngest with a knife. Mary was then subdued before she could kill the others. The slaves' owner, Archibald K. Gaines, demanded their return, but Ohio officials sought a murder trial. The fugitive slave law prevailed and the slaves were returned, but Mary Garner disappeared mysteriously while the jurisdictional dispute was still being argued. The incident had a profound effect upon public opinion in Cincinnati. One erstwhile proslavery advocate declared his conversion to the opposite position in a conversation with attorney Rutherford B. Hayes: "From this time forward, I will not only be a black Republican, but I will be a *damned abolitionist.*"[20]

Many masters made determined and expensive efforts to retake fugitives. Notices were placed in newspapers, law enforcement officers were notified, rewards were offered, personal searches were undertaken, and professional slavecatchers were sometimes employed. Fugitives were often followed into free states, although as antislavery sentiment grew, catching and returning a slave from north of the Ohio River became increasingly difficult. In 1847, for example, Francis Troutman and three Kentucky companions found six of his fugitive slaves in Marshall, Michigan, but a citizens' group prevented the pursuers from seeing a magistrate and ordered them to leave town. When they refused, they were arrested for trespassing and found guilty after a brief trial. Despite such setbacks many masters believed that a determined pursuit acted as a deterrent to other slaves. This philosophy explained why George C. Thompson was harsh toward any fugitive slaves who came to his Woodford County farm. "The rule which I have been compelled to adopt in such cases appears to be severe," he explained, "but if relaxed in a single case my place would be constantly full of runaways. It is; not to listen to their stories, but to have them severely whipped and send them right back."[21]

But other masters were not as concerned about fugitives and occasionally one seemed almost grateful to have a slave depart. H. T. Duncan of Lexington wrote a son on May 3, 1858, "Armistead is still runaway. He came home a few nights ago & took his best suit of clothes & started again. . . . I shall not trouble myself about him & care but little if I never see him again. In the future I shall sell instead of whipping. They are a great vexation & annoyance. I wish we were rid of them entirely."[22]

A surprising number of successful fugitives kept in touch with the masters from whom they had fled. When a slave girl named Milly fled she left a touching explanation for her decision. "It breaks my heart to leave you, my dear mistress," she wrote. "I shall never find so good a friend in the world as you have been to me, never any one that I shall love so much. But you have taught me many things, and among them the value of freedom. All the education you have given me has gone to make me feel that I have no right to remain a slave when I can be free. . . . I want you to know how grateful I am and always shall be for all your kindness." When Milly's master read her letter he said quietly, "I do not blame her. I shall not try to get her back."[23]

In 1846 when Cecelia, the personal servant of Fanny Ballard, was lured away by abolitionists during a visit to Niagara Falls, the young mistress sent clothing and money to her. The former slave and ex-mistress exchanged many friendly letters. In a long letter dated August 2, 1855, Fanny wrote, "You need have no fear for your freedom from me; I should never assert any claim to you if you were in my house. I tell you now that I relinquish all claims to you forever, and only hope that the fear and love of God may always be with you and that he will bless you and make your family prosper. I am and always will be a friend to the slave, and denounce the system of slavery as diabolical, at variance with Christianity." Many years later when she was destitute and ill, Cecelia returned to her old Kentucky home for succor.[24]

In an unusual case, a twenty-five-year-old slave named John Brown who had escaped from a Lexington slave jail in 1861 wrote his master a year later from England that he wanted to return home. "I am going to deliver myself up to you. I hope you won't flog me when I come to you. . . . I run away May last and would rather be your slave than free. . . . I am quite tired of being knocked about in England. I would fifty times rather be a slave than free."[25] Slaveholders were delighted to publicize such proof of slavery's benevolence.

Fugitive slaves also complicated Kentucky's relations with the states north of the Ohio River. The 1798 slave code provided for the apprehending of fugitive slaves, and the changes made in it during the rest of the slavery era consisted largely of increases in the rewards offered. An act of March 1860 provided for a reward of $20 if the fugitive was caught within the county, $125 if caught outside the state and returned to any part of Kentucky, and $150 if caught outside the state and returned to the county from which he had fled. These sums were large enough to encourage the activities of professional slavecatchers.

State laws also attempted to curb runaways by placing penalties upon anyone who assisted them. An act of 1846, for example, provided a jail sentence of one to five years for anyone who tried to persuade a slave to flee and five to twenty years for anyone who tried to incite an insurrection. A person who assisted anywhere along the way was as guilty as if he had assisted in the initial escape. Free Negroes, mulattoes, and Indians who helped a fugitive could also be whipped and were liable for the value of the slave. Other laws were enacted in an effort to cut off the Ohio River escape route. An act of December 1831 made it illegal to carry a slave across the river or to provide him with a boat unless he was in his master's company or had specific written permission to cross. A ferryman who violated the law could be forced to pay $200 to the owner, was liable for the value of the slave, and could lose his franchise. Later laws prohibited slaves from riding on stagecoaches and railroads unless accompanied by a master or provided with a valid pass.

As early as 1816 the general assembly requested the governor to seek agreements with the governors of Ohio and Indiana for the more efficient return of fugitives, and such requests were frequent in subsequent years. The existing situation, the legislators protested, was "calculated to excite sensations unfavorable to the friendly relations which ought to subsist between neighboring states." Ohio was singled out more often than any other state. But as Ohio Governor Thomas Worthington pointed out to Kentucky Governor Gabriel Slaughter in 1817, public opinion in Ohio was generally opposed to slavery, and "it but too often happens that the proofs of the right of property are defective. Under such circumstances the judges must act according to facts."[26] In 1839 a legislative delegation went to Ohio and lobbied successfully for the passage of a stronger law for the return of fugitives. Many fugitives were caught in Ohio and the other states in the Old Northwest, but the occasions when slaves were assisted in escaping made the greatest impression upon Kentucky slaveholders.

Canada presented an even greater problem in some respects, for fugitive slaves could not be extradited to the United States. The state legislature frequently requested the federal government to intercede with Great Britain for an agreement to return fugitives. Such a request was made in 1822 when the problem was described as increasing to "enormous magnitude." Five years later it was "a growing evil," but the British government remained adamant in refusing all such requests. As a consequence, the black population in Canada increased, although not as much as some slaveholders claimed, especially after the passage of the Fugitive Slave Act of 1850, and a number of the blacks were from Kentucky. While some fugitives became dissatisfied with Canada, and especially with Canadian winters, and returned to the United States, most of the fugitives who found a haven in Canada adjusted well to freedom there.

For many years Kentucky slaveholders pressed for the passage of a more effective federal fugitive slave act than the one of 1793. The 1847 legislature, referring to a recent Michigan incident in which a mob had prevented the capture of some fugitives, warned that such "outrages must necessarily result in great mischief . . . [and] terminate in breaking up and destroying the peace and harmony that is desirable by every good citizen. . . ." The demand for a stronger law intensified during the great debate that led to the Compromise of 1850. Senator Joseph R. Underwood warned his peers on April 3, 1850, that passage of a strict fugitive law was absolutely essential for settling the problems that confronted them. The South genuinely believed that it had been generous in making concessions to the North; the harsh Fugitive Slave Act was the price the South demanded for its concessions.

As events proved, the 1850 law did Kentucky and the other slave states more harm than good. Some of its provisions, such as a double fee for a commissioner who ruled that a black was a slave instead of a freedman, were so blatantly unfair that many recruits were gained for the antislavery movement, and several states passed personal liberty laws that were designed to cripple enforcement of the detested federal act. Ohio was involved with Kentucky in one of the most noted cases resulting from the act. In October 1859 the Woodford County grand jury indicted Willis Lago, a free black, for seducing and enticing a slave named Charlotte to escape from her master and flee with him to Ohio. Lago's arrest and return were demanded. When Governor Dennison of Ohio rejected the request, Kentucky sought a writ of mandamus from the United States Supreme Court to make him obey the 1850 act. The Supreme Court ruled that the Kentucky position was correct, that Dennison had no right to reject the request—but that a state official could not be compelled to perform a duty by an act of

95

Congress.[27] The *Covington Journal* declared in the November 17, 1860, issue that Kentucky might be forced into secession if the Fugitive Slave Act was not enforced. Incidents arising under the act provided excellent propaganda for abolitionists. Some Kentuckians were concerned over the inequities of the law, but ex-Governor Thomas Metcalfe probably expressed the majority opinion when he wrote a friend in December 1850 that he had decided to accept the act as it was. If the act should be repealed, "(which Heaven in its mercy forbid)—I for one will take my stand with the wronged and insulted south, and if I do not greatly err in my views, so will Kentucky with an unbounded unanimity."[28] A dozen years earlier another Kentuckian had written of the fugitive problem, "It is pregnant as I fear with the fate of this Union."[29] That danger was greater in the 1850s than ever before, as the fugitives assumed a symbolic importance far beyond the material loss they represented.

Both state and federal courts heard numerous cases involving fugitives, as well as other aspects of slavery. Joseph R. Underwood asserted in 1850, "I have never known a case of freedom or slavery where the leanings and sympathies of the judges and jurors were not in favor of liberty," but many a Kentucky black would have disagreed. Any black, slave or free, faced serious handicaps when he confronted whites in a slave state during that era, and the black who won a favorable verdict had to consider himself fortunate. Yet some cases were won by blacks and antislavery whites. For example, Ben Mercer was hired out by his owner, Joseph Mercer, to cut wood in Illinois. As a result of contacts made there, Ben was later allowed to make pleasure trips into Illinois. In 1851 a Kentucky court granted Ben his freedom because of this permission.[30] In 1850 William Hines, an agent for the American Missionary Association, was charged with helping Lewis County slaves escape. After considerable vacillation while out on bail—he said once that he did not "think he should be made a stool pigeon for the cause"—Hines returned for his trial and was acquitted.[31]

Despite all efforts to prevent them, the number of escapes probably increased in the 1850s. But the vast majority of Kentucky's slaves remained on the farms and in the towns, and their struggle against slavery was waged within that institution. At the same time, however, the slaves evolved a subculture of their own that to a considerable degree isolated them from the whites. Contacts were unavoidable, but many slaves lived largely in a world of their own that was concealed behind the ostentatious servility that appeased their masters.

After all the resistance that slaves offered and after all the efforts that antislavery groups could muster, Kentucky had more slaves in 1860 than ever before. The institution was firmly fixed in the recent constitution and the laws of the commonwealth, and every effort to establish even a modest program of gradual emancipation had been defeated. It was inconceivable that Kentucky and the other slave states would approach the twentieth century still harboring human slavery, but a solution was not in sight as the decade of the 1850s ended. Slavery was an integral part of Kentucky's social and economic system, and most white Kentuckians appeared content to accept that situation.

6

FREE AT LAST

W<small>HILE</small> SLAVERY in its various ramifications was an important cause of the Civil War, the war was not started in order to end slavery. President Lincoln was emphatic on that point. His purpose was to preserve the Union, and if he could best accomplish that by keeping slavery, it would be kept. The Republican platform of 1860 had been adamant on halting the further expansion of slavery, but it had disclaimed any intention of interfering with the institution in the states that had it. But many southerners saw in the victory of a sectional party an indication of future events. Why remain in the Union until injury was received when secession provided a solution? As late as early April 1861, however, only seven of fifteen slave states had seceded.

The secession movement and the outbreak of war created serious problems for Kentucky, with her strong ties to both great sections. Slavery was an obvious link with the South, but antislavery Kentuckians had maintained a persistent if unsuccessful opposition to slavery since the advent of statehood. John C. Breckinridge's failure to carry his home state in the 1860 presidential election was a significant indication of Kentucky's attitude. The Southern Democratic candidate lost most of the counties with the largest concentration of slaves. While Lincoln was far from being an abolitionist, he was the most antislavery of the 1860 presidential candidates. That he received but 1,364 votes in the state revealed quite clearly the absence of a strong antislavery party in Kentucky. John Bell, the Constitutional Union candidate, captured the state's electoral votes. The majority of Kentuckians were not actively opposed to slavery, but most of them, including many slave owners, were Unionists, and they returned large Unionist majorities in the legislative and congressional elections during the summer of 1861. When Kentucky's neutrality ended in September 1861 and the state elected to remain with the Union, most Kentuckians approved the decision. The typical Kentuckian of 1861 believed in states' rights, condoned slavery, and opposed secession.

As the war progressed with agonizing uncertainty, slavery became an increasingly important issue, and proslavery Kentuckians became apprehensive about its future. William Mobley, working in Laurel County for the American Missionary Association, recognized early a probable consequence of the war. "I am persuaded," he wrote S. S. Jocelyn on July 6, 1861, "from all that I know, or can learn, that it is the common & general opinion of both pro and anti slavery people that the present conflict will some how or other bring about the extinction of slaveholding." He thought that slaveholding Unionists hoped for gradual emancipation, perhaps with compensation, rather than immediate abolition.[1] Many Unionists were outraged when on August 30 General John C. Frémont confiscated the property and freed the slaves of the people in Missouri who opposed the Union. They feared that his proclamation would push the state into the Confederacy. When Lincoln ordered Frémont to withdraw his order, he explained that the policy would "perhaps ruin our rather fair prospects for Kentucky."[2]

The situation in Kentucky was calmer after Frémont's repudiation, although some farsighted slaveholders were apprehensive about the future. Numerous resolutions were introduced in the state legislature to warn the federal government against any attempt to interfere with slavery or to use Negroes as soldiers. Van B. Young of Bath County, for example, proposed: "that whenever it becomes manifest that it is the object of the present war to emancipate the slaves of the

99

Southern States, that then it is the duty of Kentucky to resist said object." Nat Wolfe, a representative from Louisville, introduced resolutions objecting to the use of Negro soldiers and reaffirming the dogma that slavery was a state matter with which the national government could not interfere. Such resolutions were warnings, for Congress had not passed laws providing for the steps the resolutions protested.[3]

Fully aware of Kentucky's importance to the Union cause, Lincoln maneuvered skillfully to prevent the state from joining the Confederacy. He was also well aware of Kentucky's divided sentiments and the attachment of many Unionists to slavery, and he endeavored to maintain good relations with Kentuckians after neutrality was abandoned. Unfortunately, some zealous Union officers did not always show the tact and restraint that the president wanted. General Jeremiah T. Boyle, appointed to command in Kentucky on June 1, 1862, soon launched a crusade against pro-Confederates that produced numerous arrests and intensive harassment, resulting in growing hostility toward the Lincoln administration. The military interfered with courts, newspapers, elections—and, inevitably, with slavery.

Fugitive slaves became more numerous early in the war, for it was much easier to slip away to a nearby Union camp or to follow a passing detachment than to flee across the Ohio. Official policy required fugitives to be returned to their owners, but enforcement depended largely upon local unit commanders and many of them disregarded such orders. As the casualty lists grew, the antislavery influence among the military became stronger and resentment against slaveholders increased. Slaves were useful for many types of military support activity, and by late 1862 and early 1863 many Kentucky slaves were being used to haul goods and build roads. On Sunday night, December 13, 1862, soldiers seized all the Negro men who had attended services at a Lexington church and put them to work the next day on military roads. Loyal owners were supposed to be paid for the use of their slaves, but payment was sometimes neglected and frequently delinquent; disloyal owners seldom received any compensation and their slaves often disappeared into the military maw. All of this had an unsettling effect on slaves. "Niggers are getting more and more trifling every day and more impudent," Alfred Pirtle wrote on December 21, 1862. "The poor miserable wretches are more bother than they are worth."[4]

Kentuckians who had been suspicious of Lincoln's attitude toward slavery had their fears confirmed in 1862 when he tried to persuade the loyal slave states to accept compensated emancipation. The president was under increased pressure from antislavery groups to abolish the institution, and his own dislike for slavery helped convince him that an attack on it might be an effective military measure. He could not afford to antagonize the loyal slave states, but perhaps they could be persuaded to take individual action with partial payment as the lure. On March 6, 1862, Lincoln sent to Congress the draft of a joint resolution: "Resolved that the United States ought to co-operate with any state which may adopt gradual abolishment of slavery, giving to such state pecuniary aid, to be used by such state in its discretion, to compensate for the inconveniences public and private, produced by such change of system." While Lincoln stressed that this was "proposed as a matter of perfectly free choice with them," there was a veiled threat in his query whether the offer "would not be of more value to the States and private persons concerned, than are the institutions, and property in it, in the present aspect of affairs."[5]

In succeeding days the president spelled out his proposal in more detail. "Suppose, for instance," he wrote Senator James A. McDougal, "a State devises and adopts a system by which the institution absolutely ceases therein by a named day—say January 1st, 1882." Then the United States would pay to the state $400 for each slave, the payments coming in twenty annual installments of 6 percent United States bonds. According to Lincoln's figures, paying for 432,622 slaves in loyal states would cost just over $173,000,000, or the approximate cost of the war for 87 days. He was convinced that such a scheme would shorten the war by much more than that period.[6]

Despite its voluntary aspect, Lincoln's plan infuriated many

Kentuckians. The state's congressional delegation protested and the press reaction was almost unanimously hostile. The *Covington Journal* of March 15, 1862, warned that "the extreme men of the Republican party are advancing step by step to the accomplishment of their long cherished purpose." The *Lexington Observer* found the plan "unnecessary, uncalled for, and calculated to do no possible good." An enraged state representative introduced a measure requiring that "any person or persons who have or may advocate the doctrine of the abolition or emancipation of slavery in the State of Kentucky, either directly or indirectly, or who sympathizes with the same, be and are hereby, disfranchised for life." Such offenders were also requested to leave the state within ten days. Despite its patent ridiculousness, the bill passed the house, 48–29.[7] When Lincoln renewed his suggestion in July, he stated that its acceptance would be a final test of the loyalty of the border states. He also reduced the proposed payment to $300. Representative Nat Wolfe spoke for the state's majority when he said, "We do not feel that our loyalty demands at our hands the adoption of the measure proposed. We do not agree with the President that the gradual emancipation of slaves in the border States would bring about a speedy termination of the war." The preservation of the Union—the purpose for which the war was being fought—was being flagrantly violated by the threats against slavery. Kentucky, Wolfe asserted, wanted restoration of the Union as it was, not the abolition of slavery. Kentucky scornfully rejected the president's plan.[8]

Kentuckians were even more upset on September 22, 1862, when Lincoln issued his preliminary emancipation proclamation that declared slaves would be set free on January 1 in those states or portions of states still in rebellion at that time. They found little solace in the fact that the proclamation did not affect Kentucky slaves; what Lincoln was doing was a clear violation of states' rights. If slaves could be freed now in the rebel states, they could be freed tomorrow in the loyal states. Coming as it did on the heels of the Confiscation Act of July 12 that authorized the recruitment of Negro troops, the proclamation stirred a storm of protest. Especially alarming was the reaction of many Kentuckians who were in the Union army. John W. Ford, a Laurel County farm boy, had enlisted in the spring of 1862 when only seventeen. He was at Memphis with the 7th Kentucky Infantry Regiment in December when he wrote: "There is a great Deal of Confusion in Camps at this time over old Abe Lincons [sic] Proclamation. If it dont stop at what its at it will Break our Regiment all to Pieces. We all say we volunteered to fight to Restore the old Constitution and not to free the Negroes. And we are not a going to do it." A few days later he voiced a suspicion that many other Kentuckians must have shared by then: "Abe Lincoln is a going to try to free the Negroes if he can and he will not Stop the war if he can help it until he accomplishes the act."[9]

Dr. Henry F. Kalfus was a major in the 15th Kentucky Infantry with an excellent record that included promotion for gallantry at Perryville. But at Murfreesboro, Tennessee, in early 1863 he and seventeen other officers submitted their resignations. Pressed for an explanation, the major replied: "My enlistment was for the purpose of suppressing a rebellion only. Since President Lincoln has seen fit to issue an Emancipation Proclamation, I decline to participate further in a war aimed at freeing the negro." Kalfus's resignation was refused, but he was dismissed from the regiment in disgrace.[10]

The ex-major received considerable public acclaim when he arrived in Louisville, for the civilian reaction to the proclamation was similar to that of the soldiers. Joshua F. Speed, a friend of the president, had warned Lincoln against issuing the proclamation. "The more I have thought of it," he wrote on July 28, "the more I am satisfied that it will do no good; most probably much harm." In the November 25, 1862, issue of his *Louisville Journal* George Prentice listed sixteen reasons why Lincoln should drop the preliminary proclamation. William T. McElroy, a Presbyterian minister in Maysville, read the document carefully and decided, "It looks far too much like abolition for me to endorse." He feared that the war would "degenerate from a lofty and noble struggle for the nation's life to a brutal war over negroes." If so, McElroy predicted, "it will be long, fatal to the country, & fail of its object." An Ohio soldier who was stationed in Frankfort in January, 1863, commented that "Union people are not so scarce as we at first thought, though nearly all oppose the President's Emancipation Proclamation."[11]

William Mobley presented a different and somewhat unrealistic analysis to the American Missionary Association. Antislavery people regretted that a clean sweep had not been made and all slaves freed, he asserted, for that step was inevitable. A moderate element accepted what had been done since it did not apply to Kentucky. "A third class, who appear to have decernment sufficient to perceive that, with slavery dead every where else, it cannot always breathe in Kentucky, are rampant in their hostility to it." In his section of the state, Mobley added, "there is a very perceptible growth of antislavery sentiment. Men who formerly declined saying anything in favor of emancipation now openly & boldly advocate it."[12]

In the definitive Emancipation Proclamation of January 1, 1863, Lincoln announced that the freed slaves would be received into the Union armed forces. Governor James F. Robinson denounced the proclamation a week later. It was unconstitutional, he charged, and inevitably what was done in the rebel states would adversely affect Kentucky. Instead of hastening the end of the war, the proclamation would inspire the South to even greater efforts. He called upon the legislature to protest the proclamation and to reject again the plan for compensated emancipation. Numerous protests were introduced in both houses, and the Kentucky members of Congress were asked to add their objections. Protests were also registered against the imposition of martial law, the "enticing away and harboring of slaves" by military units, the use of blacks as soldiers, and general violations of civil liberties.[13] As one gesture of defiance, an act of March 2, 1863, authorized arresting as a runaway slave any Negro entering the state who claimed freedom under terms of the Emancipation Proclamation. As the *Tri-Weekly Commonwealth* declared on April 17, 1863, Kentucky "does not intend that runaway slaves shall swarm through her borders."

The Unionists were in control of the state government after the resignation of Governor Magoffin in August 1862, but the unpopularity of the Lincoln administration won support for the States' Rights group. Newly elected Governor T. E. Bramlette was one of the few public figures who gave any support to the national administration, and he did so on the grounds that the sooner the war was over, the sooner Kentucky could get rid of the Lincoln administration. In his first message to the legislature on December 7, 1863, Bramlette surprised many Kentuckians by asserting, "Neither the preservation, nor the destruction of slavery is essential to our State or National existence." The danger to free government, he warned, lay "in the effort of those who would make the life of the government subordinate to the status of the negro. It is as revolutionary and disloyal to subordinate the government to the question of his freedom, as to the question of his enslavement."

Bramlette endured severe criticism because of his moderate views, and during the next year as federal measures grew even more repressive he became increasingly critical of the Lincoln administration. The use of Negro soldiers replaced the Emancipation Proclamation as the focal point of controversy, for it involved Kentucky directly, and the use of black troops would have an obvious and perhaps fatal impact upon slavery. The idea that a black could become a combat soldier challenged the concept of black inferiority that was at the heart of any defense of slavery. But the war's insatiable demand for men could not be met by volunteers when many Kentuckians were either in the Confederate army or sympathetic to the southern cause, and when the draft was put into effect it failed to produce the state's quota from among white males. The national administration saw only one solution to the problem: employ blacks as soldiers.

Kentuckians reacted predictably against the proposal that blacks be used as soldiers. Rumors circulated that entire units would lay down their arms and return home rather than endure the disgrace. Lincoln tried to soften the shock in 1863 by ordering only the enrollment of free Negroes. Although it was explained that enrollment meant listing those eligible, not enlisting them, the protests were so violent that the order was suspended until February 1864. By then the need for manpower was so great that all black males in Kentucky were ordered enrolled, slaves as well as freedmen. Opposition was so strong, however, that black enlistments were suspended in Kentucky although blacks were being inducted into military service in other border states. One of the state's most determined opponents of the program was Colonel Frank Wolford, commander of the "Wild Riders" of the 1st Kentucky Cavalry. Wolford had an exceptionally fine war record, and his loyalty and devotion to the Union had been unquestioned. But he could not accept the idea of black soldiers, and in public speeches in Danville and Lexington on March 10 he called upon the people to use force to resist Lincoln's plan. He pledged the use of his troops to block enlistments and recommended that enlisting officers be thrown in the penitentiary. Governor Bramlette was as adamant as the colonel. On March 12 he told the Boyle County provost marshal: "If the president does not, upon my demand, stop the negro enrollment, I will."

Wolford became a state martyr when he was arrested and sent to Nashville for trial. Since it was felt that a trial might result in even more public support for him, he was finally given a dishonorable discharge from the army he had served so well. Bramlette had second thoughts about the confrontation that appeared imminent, and after some mysterious conferences with such people as Robert J. Breckinridge and General Stephen G. Burbridge he called upon the citizens to submit to enrollment and to confine their resistance to lawful means. Lincoln promised a Kentucky delegation headed by Bramlette that no black would be enlisted in a county that met its quota with white enlistments and that blacks who were enlisted would be trained outside the state.

This arrangement did not produce the men needed, and on April 18, 1864, General Burbridge ordered the enlistment of both free and slave male blacks throughout the state. Loyal slave owners were to be paid as much as $300 for each slave taken. The initial rush of volunteers soon subsided, and enlisting officers resorted to intensive recruiting. Many fugitives who had sought freedom found themselves in the Union army. Kentuckians continued their vociferous protests, and soon after the November election (in which Kentucky gave George B. McClellan a wide margin over Lincoln), Frank Wolford, Lieutenant Governor R. T. Jacob, and Paul R. Shipman of the *Louisville Journal* were arrested for obstructing enlistments. After gauging the violence of the protests, Lincoln pardoned the men. The Kentucky situation was so critical that a War Department agent reported in late 1864 that a large majority of Kentuckians should be considered disloyal. The explosive situation was defused somewhat in February 1865, when the hated Burbridge was replaced by the more tactful General John M. Palmer.

Of course Palmer had to carry out orders, and he continued to push black enlistments. Volunteers increased after an act of March 3, 1865, freed the wives and children of those who enlisted. General Palmer confessed in the spring of 1865 that the army was more interested in enlisting blacks in order to free them and their families than in securing soldiers. Thus he continued active recruiting even after the surrender of the Confederate armies. By the close of the war some 20,000 Kentucky blacks wore the Federal uniform, and Kentucky slavery had been dealt a blow from which it could not recover. Although some slaves continued to be sold and some fugitives advertised for, such illusions of normalcy were just illusions. By October 1865 the number of slaves had declined to 153,000, and their $7,000,000 estimated value contrasted sharply with the 1861 figure of $88,000,000.[14] Slavery in Kentucky could not have long survived the Civil War had no other action been taken.

But action was taken that brought speedy termination to the peculiar institution. Even some opponents of slavery questioned the constitutionality of the Emancipation Proclamation and some of the other war measures that had affected slavery, and Lincoln concluded that the time had come to abolish slavery throughout the country. A constitutional amendment wa⸀

the sure way of reaching that goal, and after an initial setback the president secured the approval of Congress. On January 31, 1865, the proposed Thirteenth Amendment was submitted to the states for ratification. Succinct in its wording, the amendment was devastating in its impact upon the institution of slavery: "Neither slavery nor involuntary servitude, except as a punishment for crime whereof the party shall have been duly convicted, shall exist within the United States, or any place subject to their jurisdiction."

Some Kentuckians had recognized the inevitable end of slavery and had tried to prepare themselves and the state for that day. An anonymous "Voice from Kentucky" had written in April 1864: "Moreover, no man who is not blind, can fail to see that slavery is destined to perish as one result of the insurrection."[15] George Prentice had become reconciled to slavery's demise, and before the end of 1864 *Journal* readers were being urged to accept the Thirteenth Amendment when it was presented for ratification. But as late as January 5, 1865, Governor Bramlette still hoped for gradual emancipation followed by colonization. He suggested to the legislature that masters be allowed to hold their ex-slaves for two years while sufficient wages accumulated to send them to Africa. When the amendment was presented for ratification later in the year, Bramlette supported it. And so, to the surprise of many Kentuckians, did former governor Magoffin. Maryland and Missouri had already freed their slaves, and the number in Delaware was insignificant; surely Kentucky would not be the only state to cling to a discredited and vanishing institution.

But Kentucky did just that. When Bramlette transmitted the amendment to the legislature on February 8, he attempted to secure conditional acceptance. "No intelligent man, whatever may be his desires upon the subject, can hope for the perpetuation of slavery in Kentucky," he told the lawmakers bluntly. "Every State that surrounds us has abolished slavery. The laws for rendition of fugitives are repealed, and no possible hope of their re-enactment. The most valuable slaves have enlisted in the army or fled to other States; those that remain are hopelessly demoralized, and rendered not only valueless, but burdensome. . . . the facts exist and cannot be changed by denying them or closing our eyes to their existence. Whether the proposed amendment be ratified by you or not, slavery has been fore-doomed by rebellion, and cannot be maintained." The only question remaining was just how it should be ended. Bramlette suggested that the federal route would be the easiest, but in an unrealistic move he recommended that ratification be made contingent upon the federal government's paying Kentucky $34,179,246 (the 1864 assessed value of slaves) as compensation to owners who would lose their property.[16]

The governor's proposal had no chance of being accepted. The day was long past when the federal government would provide compensation, and the stubborn pride of the majority of the legislators was stronger than Bramlette's recommendation. A spate of resolutions condemned the amendment and called for its rejection, and both houses rejected the governor's conditional ratification. Then the house voted against ratification of the amendment, 56–28, and the senate did likewise, 21–12. Bramlette deplored their action but forwarded the rejection to the secretary of state. Later efforts to reverse the decision were defeated, and Kentucky continued to cling to slavery while the number of states ratifying the amendment moved inexorably toward the constitutional majority.

Meanwhile, what remained of slavery in Kentucky disintegrated. Inertia, ignorance, and fear of the unknown kept many blacks at home, but as an antislavery advocate admitted during the summer of 1865, "I found it not only very difficult to get the people out to work but almost impossible to get much done after they reached the fields." H. M. Young wrote his brother-in-law on December 18, 1865, "We depend entirely on hired labor, & find it is very difficult to get the Negroes so recently liberated to work at all, & then they only do half work."[17] Hundreds, then thousands, of rural blacks poured into the cities. Louisville, Lexington, and the smaller towns could not absorb the influx, and General Palmer issued travel passes to almost any black—slave or free—who requested one. Thousands of Kentucky's blacks crossed the Ohio River, thus beginning the exodus that by 1870 reduced the state's black population to well below the prewar figure.

Ratification of the Thirteenth Amendment was completed on December 6, 1865, and slavery was abolished throughout the United States. The formalities of official notification delayed the final announcement until December 18, but the impatient General Palmer issued his own statement on December 7 that slavery was legally extinct and that the blacks were protected by the general laws of the state and nation. Even then the Kentucky legislature refused to affirm the decision the nation had reached. On January 25, 1866, the house rejected by a vote of 57 to 30 a motion to ratify the amendment, and then voted by nearly the same margin that "the General Assembly entertains the opinion that the action of the past Legislature on this subject is final."[18]

Kentucky had obviously not prepared for the freeing of the slaves, and numerous legal problems confronted the government when it finally faced up to the necessity of coping with the new situation. Few masters had prepared their slaves, and many freedmen were bewildered by their new status. Harry Smith described how his master, Charles Hays, broke the news to his slaves. "One morning as the slaves were eating, Massa Hays come in an [sic] walked around the table very uneasy, and bracing himself up in the best manner possible, spoke to them in this manner: 'Men and women hear me, I am about to tell you something I never expected to be obliged to tell you in my life, it is this: it becomes my duty to inform you, one and all, women, men and children, belonging to me, you are free to go where you please!' At the same time cursing Lincoln and exclaiming, 'if he was here, I would kill him for taking all you negroes away from me.'" Then he told them to go to the granary and help themselves to what they wanted. "Then commenced a great jubilee," Smith recalled, in which Old Massa soon joined."[19]

Susan Dale Sanders was happy with her mistress, and her reaction to freedom was typical of many freedmen who had no strong incentive to leave the place of their servitude. "She told me I was free after the war was over," Mrs. Sanders recalled. "I got happy and sung but I didn't know for a long time, what to be free was, as after the war she hired me and I stayed on doin' all the cookin' and washin' and all the work, and I was hired to her for four dollars a month." This arrangement ended when Susan married William Sanders, a veteran of the Union army.[20]

Many problems remained to be solved after 1865, and many freedmen discovered that freedom had certain practical disadvantages they had not foreseen. The slave was free, but he was not a citizen in Kentucky and his status was inferior to that of whites in most respects. Many years would pass before the blacks would begin to attain any approach to equality. But the important fact was that the slave had been freed. The goal for which antislavery advocates had worked for so long had at last been attained, although freedom had not been achieved by state action as most of them had hoped. Despite the agitation of the various antislavery groups, they had done little more than keep the issue alive and under discussion during the antebellum years. They had prevented the slavery question from disappearing into quiet oblivion as the slaveholders desired, but as late as 1860 the institution of slavery appeared to be as firmly fixed in Kentucky as it had ever been.

Then Kentucky was caught up in the great sectional controversy that led to the breakdown of the democratic process and the fighting of a civil war in which the commonwealth suffered the particular agonies of a border state. The exigencies of that war brought an end to slavery in the United States, although Kentucky stubbornly refused to end it voluntarily within the state. It can be said with some truth that the antislavery movement in Kentucky was a failure. It did not end slavery within the state, and it had little effect upon the national movement. But Kentuckians can take pride in the presence of some determined citizens who continued to fight, persistently and courageously, for a cause in which they believed. Their efforts are a part of the proud heritage of the commonwealth.

Notes

Chapter 1

1. Robert B. McAfee to [?], June 7, 1841, Robert B. McAfee Papers (Kentucky Historical Society, Frankfort); George W. Ranck, *Boonesborough* (Louisville, 1901), 11, 13; Charles Gano Talbert, *Benjamin Logan: Kentucky Frontiersman* (Lexington, 1962), 1, 22, 201.

2. McAfee Papers, Draper MSS, 4CC30, May 1, 1777 (Wisconsin Historical Society, Madison; microfilm copy at Western Kentucky University, Bowling Green).

3. Ivan E. McDougle, *Slavery in Kentucky, 1792–1865* (Lancaster, Pa., 1918), 85–86; Lewis and Richard H. Collins, *History of Kentucky*, 2 vols. (Covington, 1874), 2:634–36.

4. Modified from McDougle, *Slavery in Kentucky*, 8–9.

5. Ibid., 10–12; Richard L. Troutman, "The Physical Setting of the Bluegrass Planter," *Register of the Kentucky Historical Society* 66 Oct. 1968):371. This journal will be referred to hereafter as *Register*.

6. Compiled from *Eighth Census: Population of the United States in 1860* (Washington, D.C., 1864), 180–81.

7. Kentucky, House, *Journal*, 1792 session, 7.

8. January to Breckinridge, Sept. 16, 1800, May 16, 1801; John Fowler to Breckinridge, March 5, 1801, Breckinridge Family Papers (Library of Congress).

9. Minutes of the City [Bowling Green], 1850–1860, Feb. 16, 21, 1828; Dec. 16, 1835; May 12, 1856; Jan. 24, 1861 (Kentucky Library, Western Kentucky University); Elizabeth Underwood to Joseph R. Underwood, Dec. 1, 1849, Underwood Collection (Kentucky Library).

10. Duncan Family Papers (Special Collections, University of Kentucky).

11. J. Winston Coleman, Jr., *Slavery Times in Kentucky* (Chapel Hill, N.C., 1940), 135–37.

12. McDougle, *Slavery in Kentucky*, 17–18.

13. Beaver Dam Baptist Church Minute Book (Kentucky Library).

14. Asa Earl Martin, *The Anti-Slavery Movement in Kentucky prior to 1850* (Louisville, 1918), 88–89.

15. (New York, 1931), 388–91.

16. Transcribed by Arthur Marvin Shaw, "Student Life at Western Military Institute: William Preston Johnston's Journal, 1847–1848," *The Filson Club History Quarterly* 18 (April 1944): 99. This journal will be referred to hereafter as *FCHQ*.

17. Robert Wickliffe, *Speech on the Negro Law* (Lexington, 1840), 14.

18. Coleman, *Slavery Times*, 151–54.

19. Ibid., 142–72; Coleman, "Lexington Slave Dealers and Their Southern Trade," *FCHQ* 12 (Jan. 1938): 1–23.

20. Quoted in McDougle, *Slavery in Kentucky*, 75; Rankin, *Letters on American Slavery* (Boston, 1833), 44–45.

21. *Session Laws, 1830*, 174.

22. *Turner v. Johnson*, in Helen T. Catterall, ed., *Judicial Cases concerning American Slavery and the Negro*, 5 vols. (Washington, D.C., 1926–37), 1:344.

23. Coleman, *Slavery Times*, 249–51.

24. Edd Shipley interview, U.S., Works Progress Administration, District of Columbia, *Slave Narratives . . .* , microfilm (Washington, D.C., 1936–38). When he was interviewed about 1936 the 97-year-old Shipley was still employed as a janitor in Tompkinsville.

25. Coleman, *Slavery Times*, 255–61. For a full account see Boynton Merrill, Jr., *Jefferson's Nephews: A Frontier Tragedy* (Princeton, N.J., 1976).

26. W.P.A., *Slave Narratives*, 10, 26, 2–3.

27. Ibid., 23, 47, 66–67.

28. Ibid., 2, 67.

29. Ibid., 18.

30. Ibid., 3.

31. Will Frank Steely, "Antislavery in Kentucky, 1850–1860" (Ph.D. diss., University of Rochester, 1956), 205; Steely, "The Established Churches and Slavery, 1850–1860," *Register* 55 (April 1957): 97–104; July 1849 entry, South Benson Baptist Church Records, June 1845–December 1868 (Kentucky Historical Society).

32. John B. Boles, *Religion in Antebellum Kentucky* (Lexington, 1976), 86, 90; George D. Blakey, "Men Whom I Remember," typescript (Kentucky Library), 209–10.

33. Boles, *Religion in Antebellum Kentucky*, 93, 96, 98–100.

34. *Report of the Debates and Proceedings of the Revision of the Constitution of the State of Kentucky, 1849* (Frankfort, 1849), 73; Warner L. Underwood Diary, autobiographical sketch, Aug. 17, 1864 (Kentucky Library).

Chapter 2

1. Boles, *Religion in Antebellum Kentucky*, 9; Martin, *Anti-Slavery Movement*, 12–13.

2. Dwight Lowell Dumond, *Antislavery: The Crusade for Freedom in America* (Ann Arbor, Mich., 1961), 61–62.

3. Rice's pamphlet is most easily found in Robert H. Bishop, *An Outline of the History of the Church in the State of Kentucky* . . . (Lexington, 1824), 385–418.

4. Indianapolis speech, Sept. 19, 1859, in Roy P. Basler, ed., *The Collected Works of Abraham Lincoln*, 9 vols. (New Brunswick, N.J., 1953), 3:466.

5. Evelyn Grady Adams, "Rolling Fork Baptist Church, 1788–1948," *Register* 46 (April 1948): 459–61, 473–74; quoted in Walter B. Posey, "Baptist Watch-Care in Early Kentucky," *Register* 34 (Oct. 1936): 314–15.

6. Boles, *Religion in Antebellum Kentucky*, 112–17.

7. A. H. Redford, *The History of Methodism in Kentucky*, 3 vols. (Nashville, Tenn., 1870), 1:254–59; John Nelson Norwood, *The Schism in the Methodist Episcopal Church, 1844* (Alfred, N.Y., 1923), 9–18; Boles, *Religion in Antebellum Kentucky*, 107–10.

8. Redford, *History of Methodism*, 1:267; Boles, *Religion in Antebellum Kentucky*, 111–12.

9. Boles, *Religion in Antebellum Kentucky*, 104–7; Martin, *Anti-Slavery Movement*, 21–24.

10. March 11, 1798; "To the Voter," April 20, 1798; "Attend," April 20, 1798, Breckinridge Family Papers.

11. *Kentucky Gazette*, April 4, 1799.

12. "To the Freemen of Kentucky," *Kentucky Gazette*, April 11, 1799.

13. Martin, *Anti-Slavery Movement*, 34–37.

14. J. H. Spencer, *A History of the Kentucky Baptists from 1769–1886*, 2 vols. ([n.p.], 1886), 2:17.

15. David Benedict, *General History of the Baptist Denomination in America*, 2 vols. (Boston, 1813), 2:545.

16. See especially vi, vii, 21, 45.

17. *Kentucky Gazette*, March 7, 1799.

18. Quoted in Martin, *Anti-Slavery Movement*, 49.

19. *Niles' Weekly Register* 45 (Nov. 9, 1833): 167; Martin, *Anti-Slavery Movement*, 51.

20. *Senate Journal*, 1826–1827 session, 247.

21. Alice Dana Adams, *The Neglected Period of Anti-Slavery in America* (Boston, 1908), 106.

22. Constitution of Danville Colonization Society and proceedings of meetings, May 16, 1829, to May 15, 1835, typescript (The Filson Club, Louisville).

23. *Speech of the Hon. Henry Clay, before the American Colonization Society, in the Hall of the House of Representatives, Jan. 20, 1827* (Washington, D.C., 1827), 5–13; Clay to Rev. Frederick Freeman, Sept. 27, 1837, Clay Letter (University of Kentucky).

24. *An Address, Delivered to the Colonization Society of Kentucky, at Frankfort, December 17, 1829* (Lexington, 1829), 12–17.

25. Joseph R. Underwood, *An Address Delivered to the Colonization Society of Kentucky, at Frankfort, Jan. 15, 1835* (Frankfort, 1835).

26. Underwood to James G. Birney, April 11, May 6, 1840, in Dwight L. Dumond, ed., *Letters of James Gillespie Birney, 1831–1857*, 2 vols. (New York, 1938), 1:551–52, 561–62; Jean E. Keith, "Joseph Rogers Underwood, Friend of African Colonization," *FCHQ* 22 (April 1948): 117–32.

27. Martin, *Anti-Slavery Movement*, 56–57.

28. Louis R. Mehlinger, "The Attitude of the Free Negro toward African Colonization," *Mississippi Valley Historical Review* 1 (June 1916): 295; J. Winston Coleman, Jr., "The Kentucky Colonization Society," *Register* 39 (Jan. 1941): 3–4; James T. Morehead, *Fifth Annual Report of the Kentucky Colonization Society* (Frankfort, 1834), 4–5.

29. Coleman, "Kentucky Colonization Society," 4–5; *Niles' National Register* 68 (Aug. 9, 1845): 362.

30. J. Winston Coleman, Jr., "Henry Clay, Kentucky and Liberia," *Register* 45 (Oct. 1947): 317–18.

31. Coleman, "Clay, Kentucky and Liberia," 318.

32. Pleasant Hill Shaker journal, 1853–1864 (The Filson Club).

Chapter 3

1. William Birney, *James G. Birney and His Times* (New York, 1890), 108.

2. Birney to Ralph R. Gurley, Sept. 14, 1833, quoted ibid., 128–29.

3. Nov. 27, 1833, quoted ibid., 130–31.

4. Birney to Gurley, Dec. 11, 1833, and Constitution and Address of the Society, quoted ibid., 98–109; Betty Fladeland, *James G. Birney: Slaveholder to Abolitionist* (Ithaca, N.Y., 1955), 78.

5. James G. Birney, *Letter on Colonization, Addressed to the Rev. Thornton J. Mills* (New York, 1834), 3, 7, 22, 27–33; William Birney, *Birney*, 144–45.

6. Joseph A. Borome, "Henry Clay and James G. Birney: An Exchange of Views," *FCHQ* 35 (April 1961): 122–23; William Birney, *Birney*, 146–48; Fladeland, *Birney*, 94.

7. March 21, 1835, in Dumond, *Letters of Birney*, 1: 189–91.

8. To Birney, July 12, 1835, ibid., 197–200.

9. "To the Public" handbill; *Lexington Intelligencer*, Aug. 1, 1833, quoted in Dumond, *Letters of Birney*, 1:212; Thomas Ayres to Birney [Aug. 1833], ibid., 212–15.

10. Dumond, *Letters of Birney*, 1:243.

11. William Birney, *Birney*, 183, 186, 360–61.

12. June 14, 1838, quoted in Martin, *Anti-Slavery Movement*, 105–6.

13. Nov. 3, 1838, quoted in Borome, "Clay and Birney," 123.

14. William Littell, *The Statute Law of Kentucky*, 5 vols. (Frankfort, 1809–19), 5:435-37.

15. Robert K. Loesch, "Kentucky Abolitionist: John Gregg Fee" ([Ph.D. diss., n.p.], 1969), 36.

16. *Session Laws, 1832–33*, 258–60.

17. *Session Laws, 1840–41*, 70–71.

18. Cassius Marcellus Clay, *Life of Cassius Marcellus Clay, Memoirs, Writings and Speeches* (Cincinnati, 1886), 55–57. A projected second volume was never published.

19. Horace Greeley, ed., *The Writings of Cassius Marcellus Clay* (New York, 1848), 46.

20. David L. Smiley, *Lion of White Hall* (Madison, Wis., 1962), 43–49.

21. Wickliffe, *Speech on Negro Law*, 7, 14.

22. David Donald, "The Proslavery Argument Reconsidered," *Journal of Southern History* 37 (Feb. 1971): 6.

23. Smiley, *Lion of White Hall*, 56–57.

24. *True American, Extra*, Aug. 16, 1845.

25. *Lexington Observer*, Feb. 19, 1845; *Liberator*, Feb. 28, 1845.

117

26. *True American, Extra*, Aug. 15, 16, 1845.

27. *Cincinnati Gazette*, Aug. 22, 1845; W. L. Barre, ed., *Speeches and Writings of Hon. Thomas F. Marshall* (Cincinnati, Ohio, 1858), 198–209.

28. Carter G. Woodson, ed., *Mind of the Negro as Reflected in Letters Written during the Crisis, 1800–1860* (Washington, D.C., 1926), 395.

29. Victor B. Howard, "James Madison Pendleton: A Southern Crusader against Slavery," *Register* 74 (July 1976): 195–204.

30. Martin, *Anti-Slavery Movement*, 100–101.

31. Ibid., 107.

32. Hambleton Tapp, "The Slavery Controversy between Robert Wickliffe and Robert J. Breckinridge prior to the Civil War," *FCHQ* 19 (July 1945): 163.

33. Martin, *Anti-Slavery Movement*, 125–26.

34. Clement Eaton, "Minutes and Resolutions of an Emancipation Meeting in Kentucky in 1849," *Journal of Southern History* 14 (Nov. 1948): 541–45.

35. Clay to Richard Pindell, Feb. 17, 1849, in Calvin Colton, ed., *Works of Henry Clay*, 10 vols. (New York, 1904), 3:346–52.

36. James P. Gregory, Jr., "The Question of Slavery in the Kentucky Constitutional Convention of 1849," *FCHQ* 23 (April 1949): 92; Martin, *Anti-Slavery Movement*, 130–31.

37. Hambleton Tapp, "Robert J. Breckinridge and the Year 1849," *FCHQ* 12 (July 1938): 138–43; Lowell H. Harrison, "The Anti-Slavery Career of Cassius M. Clay," *Register* 59 (Oct. 1961): 310–11.

38. Frank F. Mathias, "Kentucky's Third Constitution: A Restriction of Majority Rule," *Register* 75 (Jan. 1977): 10, 18–19.

39. Martin, *Anti-Slavery Movement*, 138.

Chapter 4

1. Mac Swinford, "Mr. Justice Samuel Freeman Miller," *FCHQ* 34 (Jan. 1960): 37–38.

2. Calvin Fairbank, *Rev. Calvin Fairbank during Slavery Times* (Chicago, 1890), 10–12.

3. This account is based on J. Winston Coleman, Jr., "Delia Webster and Calvin Fairbank—Underground Railroad Agents," *FCHQ* 17 (July 1943): 129–42; Fairbank, *During Slavery Times*; and Delia A. Webster, *Kentucky Jurisprudence: A History of the Trial of Miss Delia A. Webster, at Lexington, Kentucky . . .* (Vergennes, Vt., 1845).

4. This account is based largely upon Will Frank Steely, "William Shreve Bailey, Kentucky Abolitionist," *FCHQ* 31 (July 1957): 274–81; Coleman, *Slavery Times*, 319–21; and Bailey to S. S. Jocelyn, Feb. 16, 1860, American Missionary Association Archives (Fisk University, microfilm).

5. Wallace B. Turner, "Abolitionism in Kentucky," *Register* 69 (Oct. 1971): 337–38; Coleman, *Slavery Times*, 319; *Acts of Kentucky, 1859–1860*, 1:119.

6. Smiley, *Lion of White Hall*, 144–46; C. M. Clay, *Life*, 212, 217.

7. Allen T. Rice, ed., *Reminiscences of Abraham Lincoln* (New York, 1888), 293–94; Victor B. Howard, "Cassius M. Clay and the Origins of the Republican Party," *FCHQ* 45 (Jan. 1971): 63.

8. Unless otherwise noted, the biographical information comes from John G. Fee, *Autobiography of John G. Fee* (Chicago, 1891), and Steely, "Antislavery in Kentucky." The letter was quoted in Charles T. Morgan, *The Fruit of This Tree* (Berea, 1946), 56.

9. Fee, *Autobiography*, 29; Fee to Badger and Allen, April 1, 1846, Fee Letters (Chicago Theological Seminary; copies at Berea College).

10. Fee to Clay, April 14, 1844, Fee-Clay Correspondence (Berea College).

11. Carleton Mabee, *Black Freedom: The Non-Violent Abolitionists from 1830 through the Civil War* (London, 1970), 235–36.

12. Fee, *Autobiography*, 43; Fee's Report, American Missionary Association, *7th Annual Report* (1853), 59.

13. Rogers to President William G. Frost, Oct. 21, 1901, J. A. R. Rogers Papers (Berea College); biography of Rogers, ibid.; Morgan, *Fruit of This Tree*, 112–13.

14. Quoted in Louis Smith, "John G. Fee's Berea," Founders' Day Address, Oct. 2, 1975 (copy in author's possession).

15. William G. Frost, "Berea College," in *From Servitude to Service* (Boston, 1905), 56.

16. Fee, *Autobiography*, 146–47. There are several slightly different versions of Fee's statement.

17. Steely, "Antislavery in Kentucky," 77–79; *Kentucky Messenger*, Dec. 23, 1859.

18. Elizabeth Rogers, "Full Forty Years of Shadow and Sunshine," typescript, J. A. R. Rogers Papers.

19. J. A. R. Rogers to *American Missionary*, Dec. 28, 1859, in issue of Feb. 1860; Rogers, "The Berea Exodus," J. A. R. Rogers Papers.

20. *Cincinnati Weekly*, Feb. 2, 1860.

21. *American Missionary*, June 1860; Clay to J. S. Rollins, Jan. 13, 1860, C. M. Clay Letters (The Filson Club).

22. George Candee to S. S. Jocelyn, March 30, 1860, American Missionary Association Archives; Clay to *Louisville Journal*, March 29, 1860, in *National Anti-Slavery Standard*, April 14, 1860.

Chapter 5

1. *The Liberty Line: The Legend of the Underground Railroad* (Lexington, 1961), 35, 40–41.

2. "Rebelliousness and Docility in the Negro Slave: A Critique of the Elkins Thesis," *Civil War History* 13 (Dec. 1967): 294, 297–98, 313.

3. Gara, *Liberty Line*, 32.

4. W.P.A., *Slave Narratives*, 66–67.

5. Eugene D. Genovese, *Roll, Jordan, Roll: The World the Slaves Made* (New York, 1972), 639–40; John Hope Franklin, *From Slavery to Freedom* (New York, 1952), 206–7.

6. Coleman, *Slavery Times*, 267–68.

7. Ibid., 263–64.

8. Thomas Speed, *Records and Memorials of the Speed Family* (Louisville, 1892), 190–92.

9. E. H. Goulding to "Dear Friend," Aug. 11, 1848, E. H. Goulding Letter (University of Kentucky); Coleman, *Slavery Times*, 88–92.

10. Orlando Brown Papers (The Filson Club).

11. Steely, "Antislavery in Kentucky," 218–20.

12. Genovese, *Roll, Jordan, Roll*, 657.

13. Gara, *Liberty Line*, 36–40; Frank F. Mathias, "The Turbulent Years of Kentucky Politics, 1820–1850" (Ph.D. diss., University of Kentucky, 1966), 313.

14. Quoted in George M. Fredrickson and Christopher Lasch, "Resistance to Slavery," *Civil War History* 13 (Dec. 1967): 316.

15. Henry Bibb, *Narrative of the Life and Adventures of Henry Bibb, an American Slave* (New York, 1849), in Gilbert Osofsky, ed., *Puttin' on Ole Massa* (New York, 1969), 85, 94, 104.

16. Lewis and Milton Clarke, *Narratives of the Sufferings of Lewis and Milton Clarke . . . among the Slaveholders of Kentucky, One of the So Called Christian States of North America* (Boston, 1854), 116, 31.

17. Ibid., 7–64, 69–98.

18. Josiah Henson, *Father Henson's Story of His Own Life* (Boston, 1858); W. B. Hartgrove, "The Story of Josiah Henson," *Journal of Negro History* 3 (Jan. 1918): 1–21. Harriet Beecher Stowe wrote the introduction to Henson's book.

19. Peter Bruner, *A Slave's Adventures toward Freedom* (Oxford, Ohio, 1930), 11–45.

20. Merrill S. Caldwell, "A Brief History of Slavery in Boone County, Kentucky" (Paper read before Boone County Historical Society, June 21, 1957; copy at The Filson Club), 8; Wilbur H. Siebert, *The Underground Railroad from Slavery to Freedom* (New York, 1898), 302–3.

21. McDougle, *Slavery in Kentucky*, 59; Thompson to Letitia Thompson Vance, July 14, 1853, Edmund T. Halsey Collection (The Filson Club).

22. Duncan Family Papers.

23. James Freeman Clarke, *Anti-Slavery Days* (New York, 1883), 86–87.

24. Ballard Family Papers (The Filson Club).

25. Brown to George Humlong, March 18, 1862, quoted in Coleman, *Slavery Times*, 55–56.

26. *Session Laws, 1816*, 282; Oct. 23, 1817, Thomas Worthington Letter (University of Kentucky).

27. *Kentucky v. Dennison*, 24 Howard 109–10.

28. Metcalfe to Henry S. Foote, Dec. 1850, Temple Collection (Kentucky Library).

29. B. H. Reeves to Obid Leonard, Jan. 9, 1839, B. H. Reeves Papers (Kentucky Historical Society).

30. *Speech of Hon. J. R. Underwood on the Slavery Question in U.S. Senate, April 3, 1850*, 7; *Ben Mercer v. Gilman*, in Catterall, *Judicial Cases*, 1:397.

31. Hines to George Whipple, June 10, Aug. 15, 1850; Fee to Whipple, July 12, Aug. 9, 17, 1850, American Missionary Association Archives.

Chapter 6

1. American Missionary Association Archives.

2. Lincoln to Frémont, Sept. 2, 1861, in Basler, ed., *Works of Lincoln*, 4:506.

3. *House Journal, 1861*, Sept. 16, 119–20; Nov. 29, 341–44; Dec. 14, 457–59.

4. Collins and Collins, *History of Kentucky*, 1:129; Pirtle Collection (The Filson Club).

5. Basler, ed., *Works of Lincoln*, 5:144–46.

6. March 14, 1862, ibid., 160; Lincoln to Henry J. Raymond, March 9, 1862, ibid., 153.

7. E. Merton Coulter, *The Civil War and Readjustment in Kentucky* (Chapel Hill, N.C., 1926), 158–60.

8. *House Journal, 1862*, Aug. 27, 1007–10.

9. Ford to family, Dec. 9, 14, 1862, *Civil War Times Illustrated* Collection (Manuscript Division, Army War College, Carlisle Barracks, Pa.).

10. Robert Emmett McDowell, *City of Conflict: Louisville in the Civil War* (Louisville, 1962), 133–35.

11. Robert L. Kincaid, "Joshua F. Speed, Lincoln's Most Intimate Friend," *FCHQ* 17 (April 1943): 108; William Thomas McElroy journal, Dec. 1862 (The Filson Club); Joseph J. Scroggs diary, Jan. 30, 1863, *Civil War Times Illustrated* Collection.

12. Mobley to S. S. Jocelyn, Jan. 26, 1863, American Missionary Association Archives.

13. *Senate Journal, 1863*, Jan. 8, 719–25; Coulter, *Civil War and Readjustment*, 162–63.

14. Coulter, *Civil War and Readjustment*, 247–48, 264–65; John David Smith, "The Recruitment of Negro Soldiers in Kentucky, 1863–1865," *Register* 72 (Oct. 1974): 364–90.

15. *The Loyalty for the Times: A Voice from Kentucky* ([n.p.], 1864), 6, 22.

16. *House Journal, 1865*, Feb. 8, 395–99.

17. W. Wheeler to George Whipple, Aug. 31, 1865, American Missionary Association Archives; Edward H. Howes and Benjamin F. Gilbert, "Land and Labor in Kentucky, 1865," *Register* 48 (Jan. 1950): 29–30.

18. *House Journal, 1866*, Jan. 25, 324–27.

19. Harry Smith, *Fifty Years of Slavery in the United States of America* (Grand Rapids, Mich., 1891), 122–23.

20. W.P.A., *Slave Narratives*, 45.

A Note to Readers

THE QUANTITY of materials pertaining to the antislavery movement in Kentucky is almost overwhelming, and much of it is widely scattered in contemporary sources. Anyone intensely interested in the subject should immerse himself in the letters, diaries, journals, wills and other court records, newspapers, minutes of city councils, church records, partisan pamphlets, resolutions of public meetings, and the surviving archives of the various antislavery organizations. There is no better way of seeing how slavery appeared to the people of that era. While the notes indicate a number of sources that do not appear in this bibliography, they represent only a small fraction of the primary and secondary sources consulted in the preparation of this study.

The best study of slavery within the state, J. Winston Coleman, Jr., *Slavery Times in Kentucky* (Chapel Hill, N.C., 1940), also contains a wealth of antislavery information. In addition to many other sources, Coleman made more extensive use of courthouse records than anyone else who has written on the topic. Less complete and less interesting is Ivan E. McDougle, *Slavery in Kentucky, 1792–1865* (Lancaster, Pa., 1918). All general state histories contain sections on slavery and antislavery. A good survey is in Thomas D. Clark, *A History of Kentucky* (Lexington, 1960), while nuggets of information are scattered throughout Lewis and Richard H. Collins, *History of Kentucky*, 2 vols. (Covington, 1874).

There is no comprehensive account of the antislavery movement in Kentucky, but three sources are especially helpful. Asa Earl Martin, *The Anti-Slavery Movement in Kentucky prior to 1850* (Louisville, 1918), is a carefully researched study that has withstood the passage of six decades. The 1850s are well handled in Will Frank Steely, "Antislavery in Kentucky" (Ph.D. diss., University of Rochester, 1956), while the invaluable E. Merton Coulter, *The Civil War and Readjustment in Kentucky* (Chapel Hill, N.C., 1926), carries the story through the Civil War.

Autobiographies, biographies, and collections of writings contain much of the antislavery story. The best biography of Birney is Betty Fladeland, *James Gillespie Birney: Slaveholder to Abolitionist* (Ithaca, N.Y., 1955), but William Birney, *James G. Birney and His Times* (New York, 1890), includes a great deal of family lore. Dwight L. Dumond edited *The Letters of James Gillespie Birney, 1831–1857*, 2 vols. (New York, 1938). The most comprehensive biography of Cassius M. Clay is David L. Smiley, *Lion of White Hall* (Madison, Wis., 1962); the most recent is H. Edward Richardson, *Cassius Marcellus Clay, Firebrand of Freedom* (Lexington, 1976). Clay's own *Life of Cassius Marcellus Clay, Memoirs, Writings, Speeches* (Cincinnati, 1886), is often inaccurate. Horace Greeley, ed., *The Writings of Cassius Marcellus Clay* (New York, 1848), is helpful for the first portion of Clay's antislavery career. James F. Hopkins and Mary W. M. Hargreaves, eds., *The Papers of Henry Clay*, 5 vols. to date (Lexington, 1959–), will be the definitive edition, but since the series is only up to 1827 it must be supplemented by Calvin Colton, ed., *The Works of Henry Clay*, 10 vols. (New York, 1904). The *Autobiography of John G. Fee* (Chicago, 1891) manages to make an interesting life seem dull. A better account is Robert K. Loesch, "Kentucky Abolitionist: John Gregg Fee" [Ph.D. diss., n.p.], 1969). Fee comes alive in his numerous letters and reports to the American Missionary Association, to the journal *American Missionary*, and to such abolitionist friends as Gerrit Smith. Berea College has copies of the Loesch dissertation and of Fee's letters as well as reports from many depositories. *Rev. Calvin Fairbank during Slavery Times* (Chicago, 1890), creates more sympathy for its author than does the account of his associate, *Kentucky Jurisprudence: A History of the Trial of Miss Delia A. Webster at Lexington, Kentucky* . . . (Vergennes, Vt., 1845). Most of Lincoln's biographies and several specialized works deal with his views on slavery. His letters and messages are found in Roy P. Basler, ed., *The Collected Works of Abraham Lincoln*, 9 vols. (New Brunswick, N.J., 1953).

Too few sources show slavery as the slaves saw it, and those that do exist must be used with caution. Many supposed autobiographical accounts were actually written by abolitionists for propaganda purposes and thus are extremely biased. A number of ex-slave volumes are identified in J. Winston Coleman, Jr., *A Bibliography of Kentucky History* (Lexington, 1949). Among the most interesting accounts are: Henry Bibb, *Narrative of the Life and Adventures of Henry Bibb, an American Slave* (New York, 1849), now available in Gilbert Osofsky, ed., *Puttin' on Ole Massa* (New York, 1969); Peter Bruner, *A Slave's Adventures toward Freedom* (Oxford, Ohio, 1930); Lewis and Milton Clarke, *Narratives of the Sufferings of Lewis and Milton Clarke . . . among the Slaveholders of Kentucky, One of the So Called Christian States of North America* (Boston, 1854); and Josiah Henson, *Father Henson's Story of His Own Life* (Boston, 1858). In the 1930s a Works Progress Administration project resulted in the interviewing of several hundred ex-slaves, including thirty-four who were living in Kentucky. Almost neglected for a number of years, the interviews were published in George P. Rawick, ed., *The American Slave: A Composite Autobiography*, 19 vols. (Westport, Conn., 1972). A topical summary of the Kentuckians' recollections of slavery may be found in Lowell H. Harrison, "Memories of Slavery Days in Kentucky," *FCHQ* 47 (July 1973): 242–57. These narratives were taken from ancient memories by largely unskilled interviewers during a severe depression, and one must be aware of the tendency of many people to say what they sense the interviewer wants to hear.

Helen T. Catterall, ed., *Judicial Cases concerning American Slavery and the Negro*, 5 vols. (Washington, D.C., 1926–37), is the best guide to the role of the courts in the antislavery struggle. While the Kentucky Senate and House *Journals* do not report debates, they are indispensable in tracing the legal aspects of the antislavery movement. They also include the governors' messages to the legislature. William Littell, ed., *The Statute Law of Kentucky*, 5 vols. (Frankfort, 1809–19), and the subsequent volumes of session laws contain the results of many legislative debates over slavery and antislavery.

Slavery and antislavery have received extensive treatment in journal articles, particularly in *The Filson Club History Quarterly* (1926–) and the *Register of the Kentucky Historical Society* (1903–). A number of articles relating to Kentucky have also appeared in regional and national publications.

Many books also deal with aspects of the antislavery movement in addition to those already cited. Especially helpful for this study were: John B. Boles, *Religion in Antebellum Kentucky* (Lexington, 1976); Frederic Bancroft, *Slave-Trading in the Old South* (New York, 1931); and Larry Gara, *The Liberty Line: The Legend of the Underground Railroad* (Lexington, 1961). Two doctoral dissertations that have produced several articles were also quite useful: Victor B. Howard, "The Anti-Slavery Movement in the Presbyterian Church, 1835–1861" (Ohio State University, 1961); and Frank F. Mathias, "The Turbulent Years of Kentucky Politics, 1820–1850" (University of Kentucky, 1966).

General studies of antislavery are voluminous, contradictory, and confined largely to the abolitionist phase of the movement. Abolitionists, who in the period between the two World Wars were often described as fanatics who did much to cause the Civil War, are again receiving the praise that was common in the late nineteenth century. Excellent guides to the antislavery movement are Dwight L. Dumond, *A Bibliography of Antislavery in America* (Ann Arbor, Mich., 1961), and Merton L. Dillon, "The Abolitionists: A Decade of Historiography, 1959–1969," *Journal of Southern History* 35 (Nov. 1969): 500–522. Still useful among the older works of the modern period are Gilbert H. Barnes, *The Anti-Slavery Impulse* (New York, 1933); Arthur Lloyd, *The Slavery Controversy* (Chapel Hill, N.C., 1939); and Alice Tyler, *Freedom's Ferment* (Minneapolis, Minn., 1944). The early 1960s saw the publication of three fine works: Dwight L. Dumond, *Antislavery: The Crusade for Freedom in America* (Ann Arbor, Mich., 1961); Louis Filler, *The Crusade against Slavery* (New York, 1960); and Henry H. Simms, *Emotion at High Tide: Abolition, 1830–1845* (Baltimore, Md., 1960). The essays in Martin Duberman, ed., *The Antislavery Vanguard* (Princeton, N.J., 1965), are of uneven quality.

Betty Fladeland, *Men and Brothers: Anglo-American Antislavery Cooperation* (Urbana, Ill., 1972), and David B. Davis, *The Problem of Slavery in the Age of Revolution* (Ithaca, N.Y., 1975), place the American antislavery movement in a broader context. Fladeland asked, "Who Were the Abolitionists?" in the *Journal of Negro History* 49 (April 1964): 95–115. Ten leaders were studied in Jane H. and William H. Pease, *Bound with Them in Chains* (Westport, Conn., 1972). Abolitionists' writings may be sampled in Louis Fuller, ed., *Abolition and Social Justice in the Era of Reform* (New York, 1972). Benjamin Quarles, *Black Abolitionists* (New York, 1969), Jane H. and William H. Pease, *They Who Would Be Free: Blacks' Search for Freedom, 1830–1861* (New York, 1974), and Alma Lutz, *Crusade for Freedom: Women of the Antislavery Movement* (Boston, 1968), discuss the efforts of two special groups.

Three recent general studies are especially good: Merton L. Dillon, *The Abolitionists: The Growth of a Dissenting Minority* (DeKalb, Ill., 1974); Gerald Sorin, *Abolitionism: A New Perspective* (New York, 1972); and Ronald G. Walters, *The Antislavery Appeal* (Baltimore, Md., 1976). Among the more interesting specialized studies are: Aileen S. Kraditor, *Means and Ends in American Abolitionism* (New York, 1969); Carleton Mabee, *Black Freedom: The Nonviolent Abolitionists from 1830 through the Civil War* (New York, 1970); and Lewis Perry, *Radical Abolitionism: Anarchy and the Government of God in Antislavery Thought* (Ithaca, N.Y., 1973). Numerous articles have explored aspects of the antislavery movement as the civil rights movement has sparked renewed interest in the subject.

Renewed attention has been paid to slavery and antislavery in Kentucky in recent years.

Marion B. Lucas, *A History of Blacks in Kentucky; From Slavery to Segregation, 1760-1891* (Frankfort 1992) is now the best single volume account of slavery and antislavery in the state.

Harold D. Tallant, *Evil Necessity: Slavery and Political Culture in Antebellum Kentucky* (Lexington 2003) is an excellent examination of the idea that slavery in the state between 1829 and 1859 was a "necessary evil." Victor B. Howard, *Black Liberation in Kentucky: Emancipation and Freedom, 1862-1884* (Lexington 1982) concentrates on the Civil War aspects of the antislavery movement and the first years of freedom after the war. The vital role of Abraham Lincoln is well discussed in Robert W. Johannson, *Lincoln, The South and Slavery: The Political Dimension* (Baton Rouge 1991). The president's particular problems with Kentucky are examined in Lowell H. Harrison, "Lincoln and Compensated Emancipation in Kentucky," *Lincoln Herald* 84 (Spring 1982): 11-17, and in Harrison, *Lincoln in Kentucky* (Lexington 2000).

Slavery in the Louisville area has received considerable attention in recent years. Amy Lambeck Young, Philip J. Carr and Joseph E. Granger, "How Historical Archaeology Works: A Case Study of Slave Houses at Locust Grove," *Register of the Kentucky Historical Society* (hereafter *Register*) 96 (Spring 1998): 167-94, and Amy L. Young and J. Blaine Hudson, "Slave Life at Oxmoor," *Filson Club History Quarterly* (hereafter *FCHQ*) 74 (Summer 2002): 189-219, examined slavery on two noted plantations. J. Blaine Hudson has been active in studying slavery in the Louisville vicinity. His "Slavery in Early Louisville and Jefferson County, Kentucky, 1780-1812," *FCHQ* 73 (July 1999): 249-83, "Crossing the 'Dark Line': Fugitive Slaves and the Underground Railroad in Louisville and North-Central Kentucky," ibid. 75 (Winter 2001) : 33-83, and "In Pursuit of Freedom: Slave Law and Emancipation in Louisville and Jefferson County, Kentucky," ibid. 76 (Summer 2002): 287-325, have added much to our knowledge of slavery and antislavery in that region. He has enlarged and consolidated his studies with *Fugitive Slaves and the Underground Railroad in the Kentucky Borderland* (Jefferson, NC 2003).

Alice Allison Dunnigan gave a journalist's view of state blacks in *The Fascinating Story of Black Kentuckians: Their Heritage and Traditions* (Washington 1982). Todd H. Barnett, "Virginians Moving West: The Early Evolution of Slavery in the Bluegrass," *FCHQ* 73 (July 1999): 221-48, depicts the early days of slavery in Kentucky as does Ellen Eslinger, "The Shape of Slavery on the Kentucky Frontier, 1775-1800," *Register* 92 (Winter 1994): 1-23.

Jeffrey Brooke Allen has examined aspects of the antislavery movement in three thoughtful articles: "Did Southern Colonizationists Oppose Slavery? Kentucky 1816-1850 as a Test Case," *Register* 75 (April 1977): 92-111; "Means and Ends in Kentucky Abolitionism 1792-1823," *FCHQ* 57 (October 1982): 365-81; and "Were Southern White Critics of Slavery Racists? Kentucky and the Upper South, 1791-1824," *Journal of Southern History* 44 (May 1978): 169-90. The largely futile effort to colonize free blacks outside the United States was carefully studied in Charles Raymond Bennett, "All Things to All People: The American Colonization in Kentucky, 1829-1860" (PhD. diss., University of Kentucky, 1980). The slavery provisions in the first constitutions are discussed in Joan Wells Coward, *Kentucky in the New Republic: The Process of Constitution Making* (Lexington 1979). Edward M. Post, "Kentucky Law Concerning Emancipation and Freedom of Slaves," *FCHQ* 59 (July 1985): 344-67, explained the legal problems involved with the freeing of slaves, and Juliett E.K. Walker discussed "The Legal Status of Free Blacks in Early Kentucky, 1792-1825," *FCHQ* 57 (October 1983): 382-95. The status of Kentucky slaves (increasing in numbers but declining as a percentage of the population) is well described in Wallace B. Turner, "Kentucky Slavery in the Last Ante Bellum Decade," *Register* 58 (October 1960) : 291-307. Despite the antislavery efforts, slavery appeared to be firmly fixed in the state. We have few accounts of individual slaves. A welcome exception is Arnold D. Wax, "Robert Ball Anderson, A Kentucky Slave, 1843-1864," *Register* 81 (Summer 1983): 255-73.

Stanley Harrold has used Cassius M. Clay several times as an example of violence in the antislavery movement. Harrold moved from "The Intersectional Relationship Between Cassius M. Clay and the Garrisonion Abolitionists," *Civil War History*

35 (June 1989): 101-19, to "Violence and Nonviolence in Kentucky Abolitionism," *Journal of Southern History* 57 (February 1991): 15-38, to *The Abolitionists and the South, 1831-1861* (Lexington 1995).

The Clay-Fee odd couple association is one of his major examples of the split within the antislavery forces. Victor B. Howard, "Robert J. Breckinridge and the Slavery Controversy in Kentucky in 1849," *FCHQ* 53 (October 1979) : 328-43, found Breckinridge to be the state's most effective advocate of gradual emancipation.

The abolitionist activities of Delia Webster have continued to attract scholarly attention. Randolph Paul Runyon, *Delia Webster and the Underground Railroad* (Lexington 1996) is a good account of an unusual person. Another unusual opponent of slavery was author Mattie Griffith Brown, who left the state but continued to draw upon her knowledge of Kentucky slavery in her writings. She has been studied in Larry Ceplair, "Mattie Griffith Browne: A Kentucky Abolitionist," *FCHQ* 68 (April 1994): 219-31, and Joe Lockard, "'A Light Broke Out Over My Mind': Mattie Griffith, Madge Vertner, and Kentucky Abolitionism," *FCHQ* 76 (Summer 2002): 245-85.

John G. Fee and the Berea settlement have continued to attract scholars. Victor B. Howard, *The Evangelical War against Slavery and Race: The Life and Times of John G. Fee* (Cranbury, NJ, 1996) is a good modern study. Richard D. Sears has done extensive research on Fee and his activities. His work has produced several important publications: "John G. Fee, Camp Nelson, and Kentucky Blacks, 1854-1864," *Register* 85 (Winter 1987): 29-45; *A Day of Small Things: Abolitionism in the Midst of Slavery; Berea, Kentucky, 1854-1864* (Lanham, MD 1986); *"'A Practical Recognition of the Brotherhood of Man': John G. Fee and the Camp Nelson Experience* (Berea 1996); *A Utopian Experiment in Kentucky: Integration and Social Equality at Berea, 1866-1904* (Westport, CN. 1996). His latest work is a documentary history of *Camp Nelson, Kentucky: A Civil War History* (Lexington 2002). A lengthy introduction provides a narrative history of the camp that was of vital concern to many black Kentuckians. Marion B. Lucas has also examined the role of that camp in "Camp

Nelson, Kentucky, During the Civil War: Cradle of Liberty or Refugee Death Camp?" *FCHQ* 63 (October 1989): 439-52.

President Lincoln was severely criticized in Kentucky because of the Emancipation Proclamation, although it did not apply to the state, and his decision to use black soldiers led to near rebellion. These restrictions are discussed in Harrison, *Lincoln of Kentucky*. John W. Blassingame wrote about "The Recruitment of Colored Troops in Kentucky, Maryland, and Missouri, 1863-1865," *The Historian* 29 (August 1962): 533-45. Only Louisiana supplied more black soldiers to the Union cause than did Kentucky. John David Smith did a more focused study in "The Recruitment of Negro Soldiers in Kentucky, 1863-1865," *Register* 72 (October 1974): 364-90.

Index

Boone, Daniel, 1
Bowling Green, 56-57
Brady, J., antislavery editor, 66
Bramlette, Governor Thomas E., 105, 106, 108-9. See also
    Abraham Lincoln
Breckinridge, John: hires out slaves, 5; and 1799 convention, 24
Breckinridge, John C., 58, 98
Breckinridge, Robert Jefferson, emancipationist, 34, 54, 55,
    57, 106
Breckinridge, William L., 56
Brown, John: raid, 64, 74-75, 84-85
Brown, Orlando, and slave scare, 84
Bruner, Peter, escapee, 90-91
Burbridge, General Stephen G., 106, 107

Campbell, Judge James, 58
Canada, and fugitive slaves, 88, 89, 90, 94-95
Candee, George: at Berea, 71, 77
Clarke, Lewis, escapee, 88-89
Clay, Brutus, 3, 53
Clay, Cassius Marcellus, 3, 57; emancipationist, 48-49;
    attacks slavery, 49; slave holder, 50; and the *True
    American*, 50-53; and Mexican War, 53; fight with
    Turners, 58; 1851 election, 67; Republican, 66-68; and
    Abraham Lincoln, 67-68; and Fee and Berea, 68, 71, 73-
    74, 76-77; accuses Emily of using poison, 82
Clay Ashland, capital of Kentucky in Liberia, 33
Clay, Henry, 24; on free blacks; 29-30; and colonization, 30,
    32-33, 43, 46
Clay, Henry, of Bourbon County, 57
Coffin, Levi, and Underground Railroad, 87
colonization, of free blacks, 31-38. See also Henry Clay,
    Abraham Lincoln
Colporters, 71, 74
Committee of Sixty and the *True American*, 52
Confiscation Act, 1862, 102
Constitutions of Kentucky, 1792, 19-21; 1799, 24-25; 1850, 58-
    60

conventions, constitutional, 1792, 20-21; of 1799, 25-26; of 1849, 45-46, 56-60; Frankfort Anti-Slavery Convention, 57

Covington Journal, 64

Crittenden, John J., 64

Crowe, Rev. John Finley, antislavery editor, 28

Danville, 31, 44

Davis, Garrett, pro-slavery, 58

Dennison, William, Ohio Governor, 95-96

Douglass, Frederick, black anti-slavery leader, 35, 86-87

Duncan, H.T., 92

elections, in 1851, 67; in 1860, 78; in 1864, 107

emancipation, 45-46; defeated in 1849, 58-60. See also Cassius M. Clay; Emancipation Proclamation; Abraham Lincoln

emancipation, compensated, 101-02

Emancipation Party, in 1851: election, 67

Emancipation Proclamation, by President Lincoln, 102-4

Estill, Monk, slave, 1-2

Examiner, Louisville newspaper, 53-54

Ewing, Judge J., 10

Fairbank, Calvin, abolitionist, 61-64

Fee, Rev. John C., 57, 65; views on slavery, 68-71; and Berea settlement, 71-76. See also Cassius M. Clay

Ferrell, Landon, free black preacher, 16

Fisk, Wiley, 71

Ford, John W., 103

free blacks, 2; fear of, 29-30. See also colonization of, Monk Estill

Fry, Joshua, 31

Fugitive Slave Act of 1850, 73

Fugitive slaves, 85-97. See also Underground Railroad

Fugitive Slave Laws, 93-96

Gara, Larry, on Underground Railroad, 79-80

Garrison, William Lloyd, 34, 39, 48, 51